RUFOUS HUMMINGBIRD

MUTE SWANS

LITTLE KIDS FIRST BIG BOOK OF BIRDS

CATHERINE D. HUGHES

NATIONAL GEOGRAPHIC KiDS

WASHINGTON, D.C.

CONTENTS

INTRODUCTION

This book introduces readers to the world of birds. It answers questions that range from "What makes an animal a bird?" and "Do all birds fly?" to "Why do ostriches have such long legs?" and "How does a woodpecker find food?" The first chapter introduces the topic of birds. Each of the next four chapters features birds that illustrate particular traits or behaviors that young readers can easily relate to.

NATIONAL GEOGRAPHIC'S *LITTLE KIDS FIRST BIG BOOK OF BIRDS* IS DIVIDED INTO FIVE CHAPTERS:

CHAPTER ONE

begins the book with a look at what makes an animal a bird, as well as birds' overall characteristics. Photographs and text combine to tell the story of feathers, beaks, and feet. Types of flight are introduced, along with explanations of altricial chicks (helpless when they hatch) versus precocial chicks (quite developed when they hatch and able to leave the nest). A typical bird illustrates the main anatomy, with callouts to label and explain each part. A fun photo game that reinforces topics in the chapter wraps up each subsequent chapter.

CHAPTER TWO

charms readers with favorites among birds and the different ways they get around—flyers, runners, and swimmers—some that fly and others that do not.

CHAPTER THREE

introduces a few of the bird world's show-offs. The birds on these pages wow the reader with the ways they "talk" using songs, flashy colors, and spectacular dance moves.

CHAPTER FOUR

examines a few of the intriguing nesting habits and building abilities of birds, from sociable weavers' communal nests to a bowerbird's elaborate stage decorations to a sneaky bird that doesn't build its own nest. These pages include examples of altricial chicks that need weeks in their nest before they can fly. Readers also meet precocial chicks, such as wood ducklings, that bounce out of their nest within hours of hatching.

CHAPTER FIVE

wraps up the main sections of the book with a look at some of the different ways birds eat. Meat-eaters, fruit lovers, insect chasers, and nectar sippers bring readers to the end of the book.

HOW TO USE THIS BOOK

Colorful **PHOTOGRAPHS** illustrate each spread and support the text. Galleries showcase the diversity of related species for several featured birds.

FACT BOXES for each featured species give young readers a quick overview of the bird, including range, diet, size compared with a five-year-old child's height or hand (depending on the size of the bird), and facts about its young.

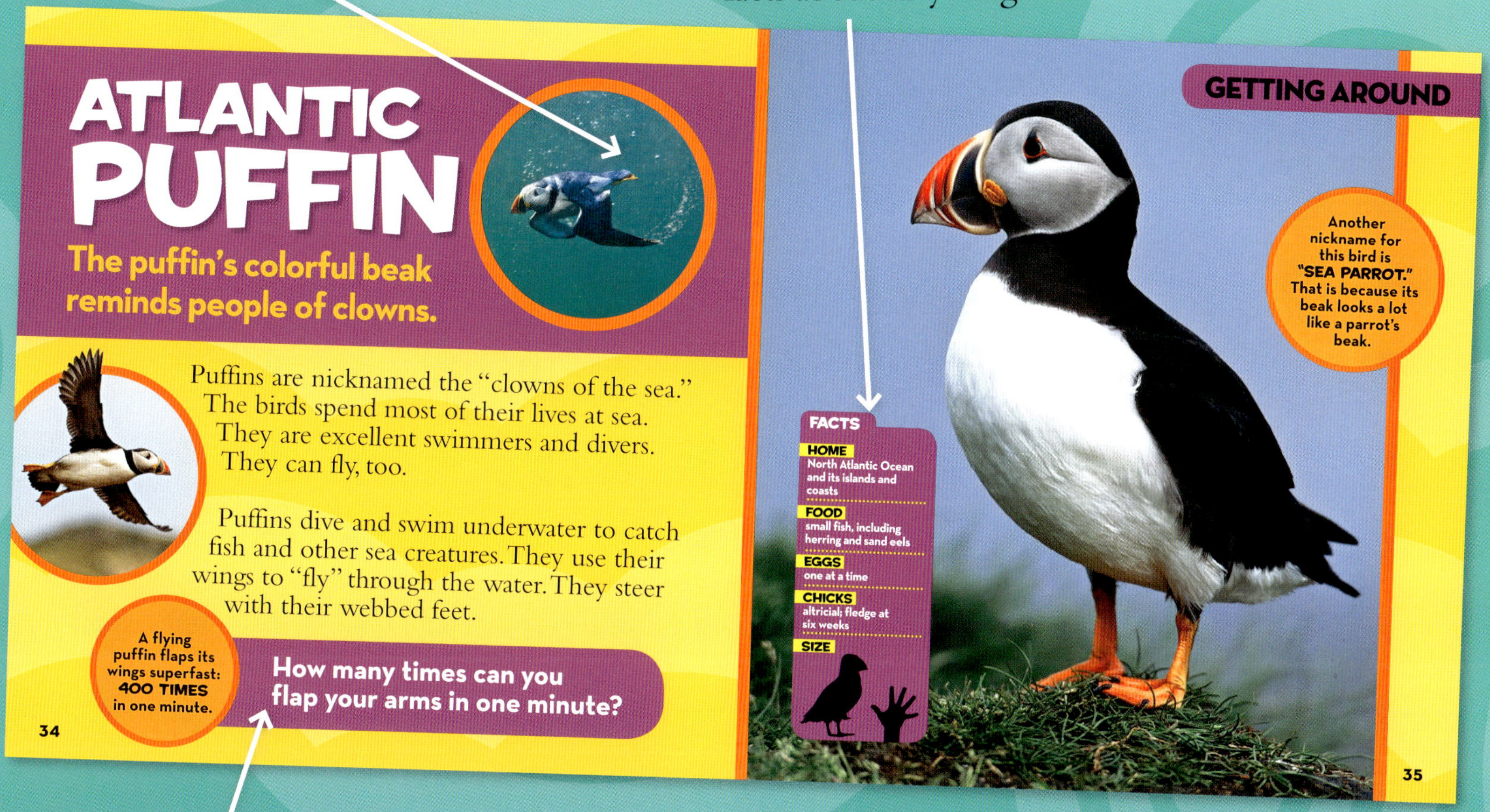

Interactive **QUESTIONS** in each section encourage conversation related to the topic.

A **GAME** at the end of each chapter reinforces concepts covered in that section.

MORE FOR PARENTS in the back of the book offers parent tips that include fun activities that relate to birds, and a helpful **GLOSSARY.**

CHAPTER 1

BIRD BASICS

BLUE-AND-YELLOW MACAW

About 10,000 different species, or kinds, of birds fly, swim, and walk around on planet Earth. In this chapter, discover what makes an animal a bird.

FEATHERS

All birds have feathers.

Birds are animals. Other kinds of animals include mammals, insects, reptiles, amphibians, fish, and more. Let's take a look at what makes an animal a bird.

No other kind of animal has feathers. So any animal with feathers is a bird. Bird feathers come in many shapes, sizes, and colors. They help birds fly, stay warm, and keep dry.

Different kinds of birds have different kinds of feathers. The way the feathers work depends on what that bird needs them to do.

BEAKS

All birds have beaks.

You can tell a lot about what a bird eats by looking at its beak. (Beaks are also called bills.) Here are a few examples of the many kinds of beaks birds have. You'll discover even more as you read through this book.

A black skimmer uses its longer lower bill to **SKIM FOOD** into its mouth as it flies just above the surface of water.

A long, skinny beak helps the collared sunbird reach into flowers to sip **NECTAR,** a sweet juice inside.

A great spotted woodpecker that **PECKS WOOD** to find insects has a strong, pointed beak.

Bald eagles have sharp, hooked beaks that help **RIP PIECES OF MEAT** from the animals they eat.

EGGS AND CHICKS

All birds hatch from eggs.

BLACK-NAPED MONARCH

Many kinds of birds are not able to do much of anything when they hatch from their eggs. They do not have many feathers. They need their parents to keep them warm, feed them, and protect them. This kind of helpless chick is called altricial.

MUTE SWAN

Other kinds of birds are more independent when they hatch. They have feathers and can walk around. Some can even swim. These kinds of chicks are called precocial.

SNOWY OWL

Eventually a young bird fledges, which is when it can survive outside the nest. Once a fledgling can leave the nest, it often still needs help from its parents, but soon it will be on its own.

FLYING

All birds have wings, and most birds can fly.

You probably see a lot of flying birds every time you go outside or look out the window. Flying birds use their wings to get from one place to another.

Some birds are super flyers. One extraordinary flying bird is the wandering albatross. Its wingspan—measuring from wing tip to wing tip—is a little more than 11 feet (3.3 m).

Wow! That means a wandering albatross could stretch its wings from one end of a small car to the other. This albatross has the longest wingspan of any bird. It spends most of its life flying over the ocean.

The **CHIMNEY SWIFT** can sleep while it's flying!

The **BAR-TAILED GODWIT** can fly from Alaska, in the United States, all the way to New Zealand without stopping.

The **ARCTIC TERN** flies 44,000 miles (70,800 km) every year.

BIRD-WATCHING

Lots of people enjoy watching birds. They are called birders, and their hobby is called birding.

Binoculars help a birder see birds by making them look a lot closer than they are.

A bird that looks like this without binoculars …

… looks like this through binoculars.

When you can look at birds up close, here are some things you will be able to see.

BIRD BASICS

BIRDS' FEET CAN TELL YOU A LOT ABOUT HOW THEY LIVE.

Ducks and other swimmers have **WEBBED FEET.**

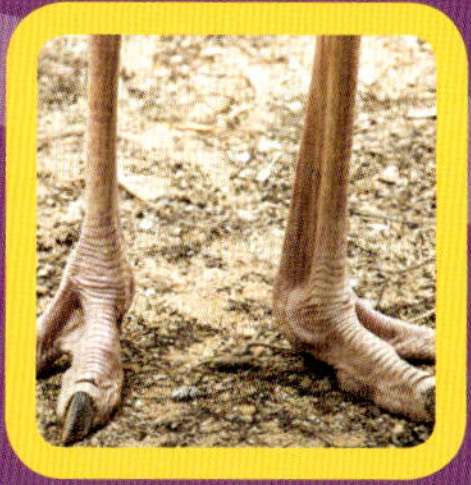

Ostriches and other birds that do not fly have **STRONG TOES AND CLAWS.**

Birds that spend a lot of time in trees have feet that can **HOLD ON TO BRANCHES.**

Birds that hunt have big claws called **TALONS** that they use to grab animals they hunt.

CHAPTER 2

FLYERS, RUNNERS, AND SWIMMERS

EMPEROR PENGUIN CHICKS

Most birds fly. Some cannot. Some birds are expert swimmers and divers. In this chapter you will read about how different birds get around.

FACTS

HOME
rain forests, woods, plantations, and city areas with trees in parts of Australia

FOOD
nectar, pollen, fruits, seeds, insects

EGGS
white; two to three at a time

CHICKS
altricial; fledge at about eight weeks

SIZE

Lorikeets have tongues with **BRUSHLIKE TIPS** that help them gather nectar and pollen from flowers.

RAINBOW LORIKEET

Big groups of these brightly colored birds fly around together.

Rainbow lorikeets are a kind of parrot.

The birds often travel together in groups, called flocks. All those lorikeets together can make a lot of noise! They shriek, squawk, chatter, and twitter.

When the birds gather in trees to eat, they blend in with the leaves and flowers around them. Their bright colors help them hide in plain sight.

There are more than 350 species of parrots.

Have you ever seen a parrot?

PEREGRINE FALCON

This bird is the fastest-moving animal in the world.

Peregrine falcons are hunting birds. As they soar through the air, peregrines hunt for smaller birds to eat.

When the bird spots its prey, such as a pigeon or a duck, it quickly zooms down to catch it.

FACTS

HOME
cities and countryside, often perching on high buildings or trees, on every continent except Antarctica

FOOD
mainly birds, some other animals (bats, rabbits, rodents, and sometimes insects, reptiles, and fish)

EGGS
milky white to brown with brown, red, or purple spots; usually three or four at a time

CHICKS
altricial; fledge at 35 to 42 days

SIZE

FEMALE peregrine falcons are bigger than males.

Can you think of any mammals—which are usually furry animals—that are hunters?

A peregrine falcon's fast dive down through the air is called a stoop.

The hunter can reach a speed of up to 155 miles an hour (250 km/h) in its stoop. That's as fast as a high-speed train.

A peregrine's **NEST** is a simple scraped-away spot on a cliff or a building. Sometimes they make a nest on the ground or in a tree hollow.

RUBY-THROATED HUMMINGBIRD

This tiny bird is an expert flyer.

The ruby-throated hummingbird can flap its wings **53 TIMES** in one second.

FACTS

HOME
woodlands, gardens, orchards, and fields in eastern North America; winters in dry open areas in most of Central America

FOOD
mostly flower nectar, also tiny insects and spiders

EGGS
white; usually two at a time

CHICKS
altricial; fledge at about 20 days

SIZE

Hummingbirds can fly backward and forward, and they can hover, or stay in one place in the air. This amazing flying helps the birds get to flowers so they can drink nectar, a sugary, sweet liquid inside of flowers.

One hummingbird might visit up to 2,000 flowers each day to drink nectar. When it gets to a flower—which is often red or orange—the bird sticks its long beak inside. Then it uses its long tongue to reach the nectar.

There are many species of hummingbirds. The ruby-throated lives in **MORE PLACES** than any other kind.

This species of **HUMMINGBIRD** is the only one that nests in the eastern United States.

What do you do with your tongue?

There are more than 350 different species of hummingbirds around the world. Here are just a few.

BOOTED RACKET-TAIL

VIOLET SABREWING

RUFOUS HUMMINGBIRD

LONG-TAILED SYLPH

BLACK-THROATED MANGO

RUFOUS-TAILED HUMMINGBIRD

TUFTED COQUETTE

VIOLET-TAILED SYLPH

OSTRICH

This bird—the biggest in the world—cannot fly.

Male ostriches make a loud **BOOMING** sound to warn other ostriches of danger.

GETTING AROUND

Ostriches are tall and weigh a lot. They cannot fly, but they can run faster than any other kind of bird—44 miles an hour (70 km/h). That's speedier than the fastest human runner.

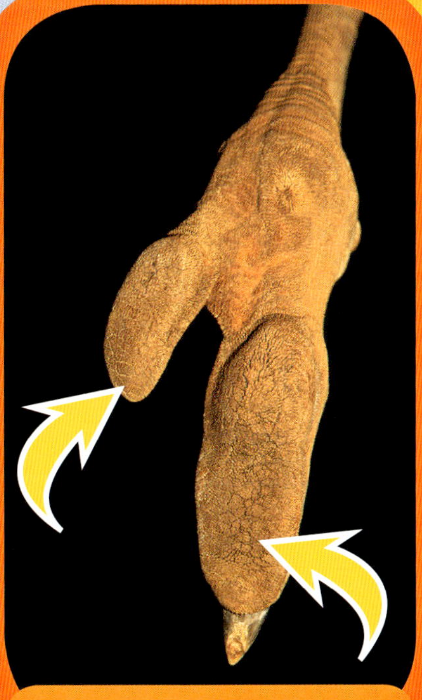

OSTRICH TOES

An ostrich has two toes. One is a tough, strong toe with a long claw. It helps the ostrich grip the ground to run fast.

An ostrich has such a strong kick that it can kill a lion.

FACTS

HOME
dry, open areas and woodland in much of Africa

FOOD
grass, seeds, leaves, flowers, fruit, roots

EGGS
white; up to 11 at a time

CHICKS
precocial; leave nest at three days old; fledge at about four months

SIZE

How many toes do you have on each foot? How many do you have altogether?

Ostriches have the **LARGEST EYES** of any land animal. One ostrich eyeball is almost as big as a **BASEBALL.**

About **24 CHICKEN EGGS** would fit inside one ostrich egg.

An ostrich **NEST** is a scraped area on the ground.

Ostriches live in flocks and share nests. One nest can have as many as 60 eggs in it.

Ostriches are one of a group of similar birds called ratites. Here are the other kinds of ratites.

KIWIS are found only in New Zealand. There are five species of kiwis.

The second heaviest bird in the world is the **SOUTHERN CASSOWARY,** which lives in Australia, New Guinea, and one island in Indonesia. There are two other species of cassowaries.

The **EMU** is the largest bird in Australia.

The **GREATER RHEA** is the largest bird in North and South America. There are two species of rheas.

A royal penguin **COLONY** can have as many as 500,000 birds. Colonies include rockhopper penguins, which are a close relative.

FACTS

HOME
southern Pacific Ocean; nest mainly on Macquarie Island between New Zealand and Antarctica

FOOD
fish, squid, and krill, which are small, shrimplike creatures

EGGS
white; two at a time, but usually only the second is incubated

CHICKS
altricial; fledge at about 70 days

SIZE

ROYAL PENGUIN

Penguins cannot fly, but they are powerful swimmers.

Penguin wings are flippers that the birds use to swim. They flap them underwater as if they are flying.

Royal penguins live in the ocean. They come ashore only to raise their chicks.

This penguin **NESTS** on the ground. It makes a simple nest of stones and grass.

ATLANTIC PUFFIN

The puffin's colorful beak reminds people of clowns.

Puffins are nicknamed the "clowns of the sea." The birds spend most of their lives at sea. They are excellent swimmers and divers. They can fly, too.

Puffins dive and swim underwater to catch fish and other sea creatures. They use their wings to "fly" through the water. They steer with their webbed feet.

A flying puffin flaps its wings superfast: **400 TIMES** in one minute.

How many times can you flap your arms in one minute?

GETTING AROUND

Another nickname for this bird is **"SEA PARROT."** That is because its beak looks a lot like a parrot's beak.

FACTS

HOME
North Atlantic Ocean and its islands and coasts

FOOD
small fish, including herring and sand eels

EGGS
white; one at a time

CHICKS
altricial; fledge at six weeks

SIZE

A puffin's beak can open wide to carry many fish at once. It eats what it catches or takes the food back to its nest to feed its chick.

One puffin carried 62 SAND EELS, a kind of fish, in its beak at once.

Puffins live at sea except for the time they have chicks. They use their strong beaks to dig burrows in the ground. Puffins make a nest inside the burrow. They use soft things such as feathers and grass to make a comfortable nest for their chicks.

Puffins gather in groups called **COLONIES** when they come ashore to nest.

Both parents take care of their chick. They take turns heading out to sea to find food.

LET'S PLAY A GAME!

Can you count the birds that cannot fly? Find all the birds that can swim. Which birds can fly?

GREATER RHEA

RUBY-THROATED HUMMINGBIRD

ATLANTIC PUFFIN

ANSWERS: BIRDS THAT CANNOT FLY: GREATER RHEA, OSTRICH, SOUTHERN CASSOWARY, ROYAL PENGUIN. BIRDS THAT CAN SWIM: ATLANTIC PUFFIN, ROYAL PENGUIN. BIRDS THAT CAN FLY: RUBY-THROATED HUMMINGBIRD, RAINBOW LORIKEET, PEREGRINE FALCON, ATLANTIC PUFFIN.

OSTRICH

RAINBOW LORIKEET

ROYAL PENGUIN

SOUTHERN CASSOWARY

PEREGRINE FALCON

CHAPTER 3

SINGERS, DANCERS, AND SHOW-OFFS

INDIAN PEACOCK

Birds can be show-offs. They sing and dance, showing off with their songs, feathers, and dance moves.

WOOD THRUSH

This bird's song is one of the most beautiful among birds.

FACTS

HOME
forests in much of North America

FOOD
insects and other small animals found on the ground in the forest, fruit

EGGS
greenish blue; two to four at a time

CHICKS
altricial; fledge at about two weeks

SIZE

A wood thrush's song sounds like music made by a flute. Males sing to each other in the spring and early summer.

Singing lets males know where others are. Each male guards a territory—an area where he wants only a female wood thrush to join him. (No other male wood thrushes allowed!)

A wood thrush is a **SONGBIRD.** Songbirds are birds that sing complicated songs. They sing mostly to guard territory or attract mates.

SONG AND DANCE

A wood thrush's territory is where a pair will find most of what they need for nesting and eating.

Usually singing is all a male has to do to tell other birds to stay away. Other males respect the boundaries.

A wood thrush can sing more than **50 DIFFERENT SONGS.**

What is your favorite song to sing?

FACTS

HOME
lakes in summer, ocean bays and coast in winter, mostly in western Canada, United States, and Mexico

FOOD
mostly fish, some other small water animals

EGGS
bluish white; three to five at a time

CHICKS
precocial; climb onto parents' backs as soon as they hatch; fledge at about ten weeks

SIZE

WESTERN GREBE

A pair of grebes dances together across the water.

A lot of birds dance. Sometimes only the male dances to attract a female. Other birds, like western grebes, dance together as a pair.

In one part of the grebes' dance, both birds run fast across the surface of the water. They do it together, side by side, looking exactly alike. This part of the dance is called rushing. At the end of rushing, they both dive underwater.

Do you like to dance?

During nesting season, hundreds of grebes might gather on one lake. Both the male and the female build their nest.

A grebe's nest is a floating pile of plant material. The birds attach the nest to plants that grow in shallow water.

Grebes catch FISH to eat. They chase fish underwater and use their beaks to either spear or grab the fish. Then they swim to the surface to swallow their meal.

The birds spend spring, summer, and fall on freshwater lakes and marshes. In the winter, they generally move to saltwater near coastlines.

RED-CROWNED CRANE

Tall and graceful, cranes dance together on land.

A pair of red-crowned cranes dance together often, especially at nesting time. Male and female cranes stay together for life once they have their first chicks.

Dancing makes the bond between a pair of red-crowned cranes stronger. Together, they bounce, leap into the air, and run with their wings stretched wide.

These birds make a loud **TRUMPET SOUND.**

FACTS

HOME
always near water in pastures, fields, coastal areas, rivers, and marshes in parts of Asia

FOOD
insects, fish, other small animals, grass, reeds, other plants

EGGS
whitish; two at a time

CHICKS
precocial; leave nest soon after hatching; can swim in two or three days; fledge at 95 days

SIZE

Red-crowned cranes can live to be **70 YEARS OLD** in captivity. Wild cranes probably live to be about **40 YEARS OLD.**

Do you know anyone who is 70 years old or even older?

MALE and **FEMALE** magnificent frigatebirds look very different from each other.

Frigatebirds make a **FLAT NEST** of sticks and twigs in low bushes.

MAGNIFICENT FRIGATEBIRD

A male shows his big red throat pouch to females flying by.

Male frigatebirds fill their throat pouches with air, making them look like big red balloons. They wave their heads, clap their bills, and shake their wings. All this showing off is for the females flying overhead.

Can you draw a male frigatebird with his big red throat pouch?

A **MOTHER** takes care of her chick for a year. The **FATHER** helps take care of the chick for the first two or three months.

SONG AND DANCE

FACTS

HOME
coastal areas and islands around the Gulf of Mexico, Central and South America

FOOD
fish, squid, crabs, jellyfish, turtles

EGGS
white; one at a time

CHICKS
altricial; fledge at five or six months

SIZE

Each female frigatebird chooses a mate from the males showing off their big red pouches. Then each pair builds a nest together.

These birds can **FLY FOR DAYS** without stopping. They can even sleep while they fly!

Frigatebirds are champion flyers. They spend their lives flying over the ocean. They hardly ever float on the water, and they only come ashore for nesting. They can soar—fly without flapping their wings very often—for days without getting tired.

Frigatebirds are usually **QUIET** at sea, but they chatter, squawk, and scream when they are nesting.

The **TURQUOISE COLOR** on this bird's head is bare skin, not feathers.

FACTS

HOME
forest on two islands in Indonesia

FOOD
mostly fruit, also insects

EGGS
whitish; one or two at a time

CHICKS
altricial; fledge at 20 to 30 days

SIZE

WILSON'S BIRD-OF-PARADISE

Colorful feathers and fancy dancing help the male attract a mate.

A male Wilson's bird-of-paradise gets ready to dance for a female. First, he clears an area on the forest floor.

This area, where he will dance, is called an arena. He moves all the fallen leaves and other plants from his arena.

When a female comes to watch his dance—called a display—he shows off all his colorful feathers. He bows and bends to make sure she sees all his beautiful colors.

As he **DISPLAYS,** the male Wilson's bird-of-paradise also sings and calls with whistlelike chirping sounds.

There are 39 different species of birds-of-paradise. Here are just a few.

SPLENDID ASTRAPIA

PARADISE RIFLEBIRD

Which bird-of-paradise is your favorite? Why?

STEPHANIE'S ASTRAPIA

RED BIRD-OF-PARADISE

GREATER BIRD-OF-PARADISE

KING BIRD-OF-PARADISE

WESTERN PAROTIA

BLUE BIRD-OF-PARADISE

TWELVE-WIRED BIRD-OF-PARADISE

LET'S PLAY A GAME!

A pattern is something that repeats. The birds make three patterns in the three rows in this game. Can you say which bird belongs in each of the three empty circles?

2 HARDER

RED-CROWNED CRANE

MAGNIFICENT FRIGATEBIRD

WOOD THRUSH

RED-CROWNED CRANE

MAGNIFICENT FRIGATEBIRD

3 HARDEST

WILSON'S BIRD-OF-PARADISE

RED-CROWNED CRANE

WILSON'S BIRD-OF-PARADISE

MAGNIFICENT FRIGATEBIRD

WILSON'S BIRD-OF-PARADISE

SONG AND DANCE

1 EASY

WOOD THRUSH

WESTERN GREBE

WOOD THRUSH

WESTERN GREBE

?

WOOD THRUSH

RED-CROWNED CRANE

MAGNIFICENT FRIGATEBIRD

WOOD THRUSH

?

RED-CROWNED CRANE

WILSON'S BIRD-OF-PARADISE

MAGNIFICENT FRIGATEBIRD

WILSON'S BIRD-OF-PARADISE

?

CHAPTER 4

BUILDERS, WEAVERS, AND NESTERS

WHITE STORKS

In this chapter, you will see some amazing ways that birds build nests and raise their chicks.

Seven states name the northern cardinal as their **STATE BIRD:** Illinois, Indiana, Kentucky, North Carolina, Ohio, Virginia, and West Virginia.

FACTS

HOME
gardens and dense, shrubby areas in much of eastern North America and in Texas and the desert Southwest

FOOD
seeds, fruit, insects

EGGS
whitish speckled with gray or brown; two to five at a time

CHICKS
altricial; fledge at about ten days

SIZE

NORTHERN CARDINAL

Bright red male cardinals are easy to see on a winter day.

Male cardinals get along with each other during the winter. They are not as friendly in the springtime.

The female cardinal does most of the **NESTBUILDING.** She uses twigs, leaves, bark, weeds, grasses, roots, and pine needles.

Spring is when cardinal pairs build their nests. They do not want other pairs in the same area. So males fight each other if one gets too close to another cardinal's nesting area.

Cardinals incubate, or sit on their eggs to keep them safe and warm, for almost two weeks before they hatch. The mother cardinal does most of the incubating, but both parents feed the chicks when they hatch.

A cardinal's **SONGS** sound like *cheer, cheer, cheer* and also *birdie, birdie, birdie.*

Female cardinals are not as brightly colored as the males. They are mostly golden brown but have some red in their wings, tail, and head.

Both males and females have feathers on the tops of their heads that form a crest. The crest sticks up when the birds are excited. The crest flattens when the birds are calm.

Have you ever made a crest on your head with shampoo bubbles?

Sometimes two male cardinals fight over **FOOD.** The faster bird flies away with the snack.

HOUSE SPARROW

These noisy birds like to live near people.

FACTS

HOME
found on every continent except Antarctica, wherever people live

FOOD
grains, seeds, insects, people's leftover food

EGGS
greenish or bluish white with brown or gray spots; usually three to five at a time

CHICKS
altricial; fledge at about two weeks

SIZE

The male house sparrow with the biggest black patch on his throat tends to be the "**BOSS**" of other sparrows in his flock.

House sparrows are not **SHY.** They come right up to you, hoping you will toss them something to eat.

House sparrows live near people. They make nests in all sorts of things that people have built.

Some sparrows build nests inside traffic lights. Others build them in the walls of houses.

You have probably seen house sparrows. They follow lawn mowers to catch the insects the mower stirs up.

Sparrows hop around near people in city parks, waiting for crumbs. They take dust baths in dirt in yards and splash in puddles on driveways.

Have you ever seen a bird take a bath in dust or in a puddle of water?

SOCIABLE WEAVER

These weavers build huge, connected nests where many families live.

Weavers get all the **WATER** they need from the insects they eat.

Sociable weavers live in big flocks. The nests they build are big and last a long time. No other birds make such big connected nests.

Weavers make their nests around a strong branch, a tree trunk, or even a telephone pole. The birds use twigs and dry grasses to build the nests, which look like haystacks up in the tree.

The birds use their **NEST** over and over. Sometimes other kinds of birds live in weaver nests, too.

Some sociable weaver **NESTS** have been used for a hundred years.

FACTS

HOME
deserts and other dry areas in southern Africa

FOOD
mostly insects; also seeds, bark, leaves

EGGS
white with gray speckles; two to six at a time

CHICKS
altricial; fledge at 20 to 24 days

SIZE

These huge nests have entrance holes that lead into the part where each pair of birds lives.

Their nests have chambers, or rooms, of different temperatures. The chambers in the middle are warm. That is where the birds sleep at night when it is cold outside. The outer chambers give the birds cool shelter during the hot daytime.

Would you rather play outside when it is hot or when it is cold?

RUFOUS HORNERO

These birds use mud to make big oven-shaped nests.

FACTS

HOME
open areas in eastern parts of South America

FOOD
insects, spiders, seeds, fruit

EGGS
dull white with lots of dark brown speckles; three or four at a time

CHICKS
altricial; fledge in 24 to 26 days

SIZE

Old-fashioned outdoor ovens looked a lot like the nest of an hornero. These birds are also called ovenbirds.

It can take a male and female pair months to build the nest where the female will lay her eggs.

OUTDOOR OVEN

The mud that the birds use dries in the sun and becomes hard. Sometimes they mix in straw, grass, or hair to make the mud nest stronger.

Rufous hornero **NESTS** can be seen on big tree branches, tree stumps, rocks, and even on telephone poles and people's houses.

Horneros only use their nests **ONCE.** But the nests last for years, so other kinds of birds use them when the horneros are finished.

The nest's entrance hole leads to a hallway. At the end of the hall is the chamber where the female lays her eggs. The parents line that part of the nest with soft things like grass or leaves.

Have you ever played in a mud puddle?

FACTS

HOME
mountain rain forest in New Guinea

FOOD
fruit, insects

EGGS
white; one at a time

CHICKS
altricial; fledge at about three weeks

SIZE

VOGELKOP BOWERBIRD

The male bowerbird uses decorations to attract a female mate.

Instead of beautiful feathers to make a female pay attention to him, the Vogelkop bowerbird makes a bower—a sort of stage where he puts on a show.

SAY MY NAME: VO-gull-kop

First, he picks a small tree to use as the center of his bower. He makes a roof of stems that reaches from the tree to the ground. Then he makes a carpet of moss in front.

The bowerbird decorates the area with flowers, insect wings, fruits, and other colorful or shiny things he finds in the forest. Each male has a different decorating style.

Red, blue, black, and orange are the Vogelkop bowerbird's favorite **COLORS** for decorating his bower.

The **FEMALE** bowerbird makes a messy nest of sticks lined with leaves in a tree. She then lays her egg. The female takes care of her chick by herself.

When a male bowerbird finishes his bower, he starts calling to females. He wants one to decide his is her favorite **ART GALLERY.**

If you were a bowerbird, what would you use to decorate your bower?

A female visits several bowers. When she decides which one she likes best, she picks that bowerbird to be her mate.

BARN SWALLOW

These swallows build nests of mud in buildings made by people.

These birds swoop and twist and turn as they follow **INSECTS** to catch them in the air.

Before there were buildings made by humans, barn swallows made their nests in **CAVES.**

Barn swallows collect **MUD** in their beaks for their nest.

BUILDING & NESTING

Barn swallows almost always make their nests in places like barns, sheds, or bridges. The male and female work together to build a nest.

The birds collect mud from mud puddles or sides of streams. Sometimes they mix the mud with grass.

FACTS

HOME
open areas, countryside, and near water across most of the world

FOOD
insects that they catch as they fly

EGGS
white with brown, lavender, and gray spots; three to seven at a time

CHICKS
altricial; fledge at about three or four weeks

SIZE

Have you ever worked with a friend to build or make something?

Barn swallows build a flat platform first. Then they build up the sides of the nest.

When the mud part of the nest is done, the birds line the inside with grass and feathers. Then the mother lays her eggs, which hatch in about two weeks.

WOOD DUCK

Here's a duck with claws that help it grip tree branches.

Wood ducks live in woodlands near water. They are comfortable in trees. Most other ducks are not. Wood ducks can perch, or stand, on a tree branch because of their special feet. Their wings are short, so they can easily avoid trees and branches as they fly.

Wood ducks do not **QUACK.** They squeak, whistle, and squawk.

FACTS

HOME
wet areas with trees for nesting in much of North America

FOOD
seeds, fruits, nuts, plants, insects, snails

EGGS
white or tan; 6 to 16 eggs at a time

CHICKS
precocial; swim at a day old; fledge at 56 to 70 days

SIZE

Wood ducks nest in holes called cavities high up in trees. They cannot make a cavity themselves. They look for a place where part of a tree has rotted away, leaving a cavity.

The female wood duck is not as **COLORFUL** as the male. Her brown color helps her hide from any predators—animals that might hunt for ducks to eat—while she is taking care of her eggs and ducklings.

Have you ever seen a duck?

The mother duck lines a nest inside the cavity with soft feathers. She lays her eggs. A day after the ducklings hatch, their mother calls them to leave the nest.

The ducklings jump to her on the ground or water below. Sometimes they jump from a nest that is as high up as a five-story building. The ducklings don't get hurt. They are so fluffy and light that they bounce.

People often make **NEST BOXES** for wood ducks to use.

If the nest is not over water, the mother leads her ducklings to a nearby creek or pond.

BALD EAGLE

The bald eagle makes the biggest single nest of any kind of bird.

This bird is not really **BALD.** It has feathers on its head. "Bald" is an old word that used to mean "white."

If you could give the bald eagle a new name, what would you call it?

BUILDING & NESTING

A pair of bald eagles usually stays together for life. They build a nest of sticks in a large tree and add to it year after year.

It gets bigger and bigger. They line it with plants like moss, seaweed, and grass.

Over the years, a bald eagle nest can grow so big that a medium-size car could fit inside it!

FACTS

HOME
forests near lakes, rivers, marshes, and coasts in much of North America

FOOD
mainly fish, also birds, other animals, and carrion—animals that are already dead

EGGS
white; one to three at a time

CHICKS
altricial; fledge at about 80 days

SIZE

The bald eagle is a **NATIONAL SYMBOL** of the United States.

AUSTRALIAN BRUSH-TURKEY

This bird builds a nest that keeps its eggs warm.

FACTS

HOME
rain forest and dry, scrubby coastal areas in eastern Australia

FOOD
insects, seeds, fruit

EGGS
white; one at a time

CHICKS
superprecocial

SIZE

Australian brush-turkeys do not incubate their eggs by sitting on them. It is their special nest that keeps eggs the right temperature.

The male brush-turkey gathers a huge pile of dead leaves and other plant material he finds on the ground. He uses his big feet to rake the vegetation together and shape the mound.

The Australian brush-turkey is not related to the **TURKEYS** many Americans eat on Thanksgiving Day.

When the nest is finished, several female brush-turkeys come by to lay eggs in the mound. Then the male covers up all the eggs.

The nest stays warm inside. As the plant material rots, it makes heat. The sun helps warm things up, too.

The brush-turkey is a kind of bird called a **MEGAPODE.** That word means "large foot." The birds have big feet.

There are two other megapodes in Australia. They are the **ORANGE-FOOTED SCRUBFOWL** and the **MALLEEFOWL.**

Only the male takes care of the nest. He makes sure it stays the right temperature. He feels the temperature inside by digging a little hole and sticking his beak into the mound. If the temperature gets too hot, he takes vegetation away to cool off the inside of the mound. If the temperature gets too cool, he adds vegetation to create more heat.

When the chicks hatch, they break out of their eggshells with their strong claws. Then the chicks scratch their way out of the mound.

Chicks hatch ready to run around and look for food right away. They have feathers when they hatch, and a few hours later, the chicks can fly. They do not need their parents to take care of them.

What are three things you could do as soon as you were born?

COMMON CUCKOO

This sneaky bird lays her eggs in the nests of other birds.

CUCKOO EGG

The cuckoo gets other birds to raise her chicks. She sneaks an egg into another bird's nest, and then another egg into another nest, and so on.

The sneaky cuckoo waits until parents leave their nest. She swoops in and kicks out one of the eggs from the nest. She lays her own egg in its place. Her egg looks a lot like the eggs of the birds she tricks.

A bird that lays its egg in another bird's nest is called a **BROOD PARASITE.**

The cuckoo **MIGRATES** south to Africa for the winter and returns to Europe in the spring.

The cuckoo egg usually hatches before the others. As soon as it does, the cuckoo chick kicks out the other eggs. The birds that built the nest feed the cuckoo. They do not realize it is not their own chick.

By the time the cuckoo is ready to fly away, it is bigger than the parents that fed it.

FACTS

HOME
forests and wetlands in much of Africa, Europe, and Asia

FOOD
insects (they love caterpillars), worms, spiders

EGGS
vary in color and may be spotted or solid; up to 12 laid in 12 different nests over a year

CHICKS
altricial; fledge at about three weeks

SIZE

The **CUCKOO'S CALL** sounds like its name: *cuck-oo, cuck-oo!*

Have you ever seen or heard of a cuckoo clock?

LET'S PLAY A GAME!

Help the barn swallow, sociable weaver, and rufous hornero each get back to the right nest. Follow the correct paths with your finger.

BARN SWALLOW

SOCIABLE WEAVER

RUFOUS HORNERO

NEST

NEST

NEST

CHAPTER 5

HUNTERS, GATHERERS, AND SCAVENGERS

BARN OWL

It is time to eat for the birds in this chapter. From fish to mice to bugs to fruit, you will see lots of ways birds find food.

AMERICAN WHITE PELICAN

A pelican has a big throat pouch that it uses to hold fish.

FACTS

HOME
mostly freshwater wetlands, lakes, and rivers, and sometimes saltwater, in north-central North America; winters in southern parts of North America, mostly along the coast

FOOD
mostly fish, also salamanders, crayfish

EGGS
white; two at a time

CHICKS
altricial; fledge at about ten weeks

SIZE

White pelicans are water birds. To eat, they swim along the surface of water in a lake, a river, or the ocean.

This bird is one of the **HEAVIEST** flying birds.

TIME TO EAT

A pelican dips its huge orange bill into the water to scoop up fish. The pouch in its throat stretches as it fills with water and fish.

The pelican lets the water drain out of the pouch. It swallows the fish left behind.

What do you use to carry a lot of things at once?

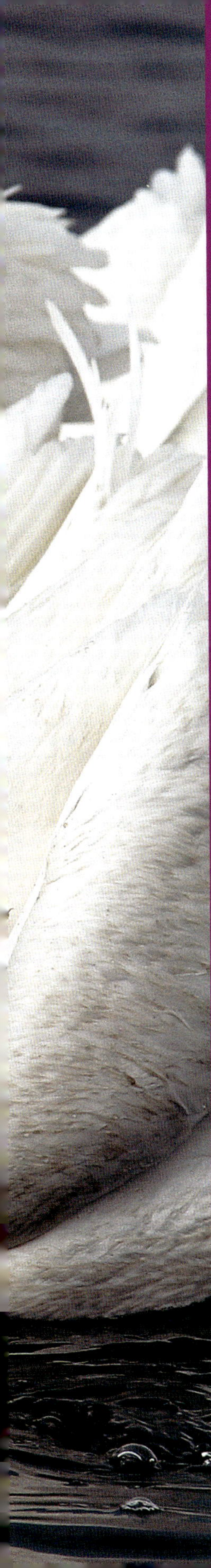

Pelicans often work together to catch food. First, they line up. Then they swim toward shallow water, trapping fish in front of the line. Sometimes they trap fish by forming a circle.

White pelicans do not carry fish in their **POUCHES** when flying.

A flock of pelicans forms a **V-SHAPE** as it flies.

They flap their wings slowly and spend most of the time in the air **SOARING**—flying without flapping.

SNOWY OWL

These owls hunt during the day.

FACTS

HOME
northern parts of North America, Europe, and Asia

FOOD
mainly lemmings; also birds and other small animals

EGGS
white; 3 to 11 at a time

CHICKS
altricial; fledge at around 20 days

SIZE

Many kinds of owls hunt at night, but the snowy owl looks for food during the day. They use fences, mounds on the ground, sand dunes, and hay bales as good spots to watch around them for prey, or animals they hunt.

Their favorite food is lemmings. Lemmings are small, mouselike animals.

A snowy owl can eat 1,600 **LEMMINGS** each year.

Why do you think this owl has "snowy" in its name?

To catch a lemming, a snowy owl must be patient. It might sit in one spot for hours. It listens and watches. When it sees or hears its prey, the owl runs or flies over to pounce on its meal.

There are about 230 species of owls around the world. The snowy owl is one of 19 species found in North America. Here are a few more owls found in North America.

GREAT GRAY OWLS are very large owls. Females are usually bigger than males—as long as three of these books end to end.

BURROWING OWLS are small—each owl is only ten inches (25 cm) tall. That is about the height of this book. Burrowing owls nest in the ground.

GREAT HORNED OWLS are big, heavy owls that have long tufts of feathers on the tops of their heads. The tufts look like horns. This owl is nocturnal, which means it is awake at night and rests during the day.

BARN OWLS live in more parts of the world than any other species of owl. They have heart-shaped faces. Barn owls don't hoot like many other owls do. They scream.

EASTERN SCREECH-OWLS are comfortable living in more kinds of areas than any other North American owl. These owls live in forests and woods, parks, and, as long as there are trees, in big cities and little towns.

PILEATED WOODPECKER

This woodpecker pecks holes in trees with its beak.

Pileated woodpeckers eat lots of carpenter ants. These ants live under tree bark in rotting wood.

Woodpeckers use their sharp beaks to peck away at the wood to find yummy ants to eat underneath.

TIME TO EAT

FACTS

HOME
forests and woods with big trees throughout much of northern and eastern North America

FOOD
mainly carpenter ants, also other insects, fruits, nuts

EGGS
white; three to five at a time

CHICKS
altricial; fledge at about 28 days

SIZE

Where do you think a good place would be to go to hear a woodpecker pecking?

A pileated woodpecker may make huge holes as it follows **CARPENTER ANT TUNNELS** under tree bark.

You can tell a pileated woodpecker was pecking at a tree if you see holes that are **SHAPED LIKE RECTANGLES.**

Rat-a-tat-tat! A woodpecker hammers into the wood. It pulls back its head using its long neck. Then it zooms its head forward, hitting the tree with its strong bill.

All along, it clings tightly to the side of the tree with its feet. Big chunks of wood fall to the ground. The woodpecker finds and gobbles up the insects in the tree.

AMERICAN ROBIN

Robins eat lots of earthworms during the spring and summer.

Only robins that live in the far, cold north **FLY SOUTH** to spend winter where it is warmer.

Robins usually gather in big flocks in the winter. They roost, or rest, together in trees. They eat berries and other fruits they find in trees and bushes.

They also eat earthworms. A robin hops across the ground. Suddenly, it stops. It tilts its head to the side as it spots a worm.

A robin's **SONG** sounds like it is saying ***cheerily, cheer up, cheer up, cheerily, cheer up!***

FACTS

HOME
lawns, fields, parks, woods, and forests in most of North America

FOOD
worms, fruit, insects, seeds, snails

EGGS
blue; three to five at a time

CHICKS
altricial; fledge at about 13 days

SIZE

Have you ever dug in dirt and found an earthworm?

The bird quickly grabs the worm with its beak and tugs it out of the ground. Breakfast!

Maybe you have seen a robin looking for earthworms. If you spot a robin running quickly across the ground, keep watching to see whether it catches a worm.

FACTS

HOME
forests, woodlands, parks, and suburbs in eastern Canada and United States

FOOD
fruits, nuts, seeds, insects, small animals such as frogs and mice

EGGS
blue, green, or yellow with brown or gray spots; three to six at a time

CHICKS
altricial; fledge at about three weeks

SIZE

To eat an acorn, a jay holds it with its **FEET.** Then it pecks the acorn open with its beak.

Blue jays have crests. Can you think of one other bird in this book that has a crest?

BLUE JAY

These birds love to eat acorns.

Blue jays **SING** using soft clicks, whines, whirs, and other noises that can last more than two minutes.

In the fall, blue jays hide acorns to eat during the winter.

A blue jay can carry five acorns at a time. It can hold three inside its throat in a special pouch. At the same time, it carries a fourth acorn in its mouth and a fifth one with the tip of its beak.

A blue jay hides up to **5,000 ACORNS** in a season.

The bird hides the acorns on the ground—under rocks and bushes and in soft dirt. If the blue jay does not come back to eat an acorn during the winter, it can grow into an oak tree. So blue jays are good tree planters!

RED-BILLED OXPECKER

These birds ride on zebras and other animals.

FACTS

HOME
grasslands in much of eastern and southern Africa

FOOD
mostly ticks, also termites

EGGS
white with brown speckles; two to five at a time

CHICKS
altricial; fledge at about two months

SIZE

Oxpeckers are also called **TICKBIRDS.**

Red-billed oxpeckers live in the grasslands of Africa, where they find their favorite food. They love to eat ticks.

A tick is a pesky bug that drinks blood from the animal it attaches itself to. Zebras and other animals often have ticks on them.

As an oxpecker **EATS TICKS** off a zebra, it also cleans blood and dirt away from the little cut made by the tick, which may help the zebra's skin heal.

Oxpeckers pick ticks off the bodies of the animals they land on. Zebras, rhinoceroses, and other animals don't mind the birds at all. The birds help them by getting rid of the pesky ticks.

If you were a zebra, would you be happy to have oxpeckers on your head?

A toucan's **BILL** can grow to be a third of the length of the entire bird.

The keel-billed toucan is the national bird of the country of **BELIZE,** in Central America.

KEEL-BILLED TOUCAN

The toucan can reach fruit with its long beak.

FACTS

HOME
rain forests from southern Mexico to parts of South America

FOOD
mostly fruit, also bird eggs, insects, small lizards, frogs, chicks

EGGS
shiny white; two to four at a time

CHICKS
altricial; fledge at eight to nine weeks

SIZE

The keel-billed toucan eats fruit in the rain forests where it lives. Often the fruit grows on little twigs that cannot hold the weight of the big bird. So the toucan uses the tip of its long beak to pick the fruit. Then it tosses back its head and gulps it down whole.

The toucan's **LONG TONGUE** has the shape and look of a feather.

Toucans are important to the rain forest. The seeds in the fruits they eat get carried inside them to other parts of the forest.

Keel-billed toucans hang around in **FLOCKS** of up to 12 birds.

After toucans swallow fruit, they throw up big seeds or poop out smaller seeds as they move around the forest. Those seeds fall to the ground and then can grow to become new trees.

What is your favorite kind of fruit?

KING VULTURE

Vultures are an important part of nature's cleanup crew.

King vultures have **HOOK-SHAPED BEAKS** with sharp edges that are strong enough to tear through tough meat.

When animals die, their bodies become food for other animals. King vultures, and other animals that eat animals they did not kill themselves, are called scavengers.

King vultures soar through the air, looking down for dead animals, called carrion. They help keep nature clean by getting rid of rotting meat full of germs.

What do you use to cut up your food?

Their wings are so long that these birds do not flap very much. They **SOAR** like kites.

FACTS

HOME
forests and nearby grasslands from Mexico to Argentina

FOOD
carrion

EGGS
creamy white; one at a time

CHICKS
altricial; fledge at about three months

SIZE

The vulture's head is brightly colored. It is bare skin, not feathers, that is colorful. Scientists think they have bare heads so that it is easier for the birds to stay clean. Germs from their yucky food would get stuck in feathers.

LET'S PLAY A GAME!

Help these birds find their favorite meals! Match each food with the bird that eats it.

- FISH
- LEMMING
- ANT
- WORM
- ACORN
- TICK
- FRUIT
- CARRION

ANSWERS: PELICAN/FISH; OWL/LEMMING; WOODPECKER/ANT; ROBIN/WORM; BLUE JAY/ACORN; OXPECKER/TICK; TOUCAN/FRUIT; VULTURE/CARRION

KING VULTURE

RED-BILLED OXPECKER

PILEATED WOODPECKER

KEEL-BILLED TOUCAN

BLUE JAY

BIRD MAP

Use this world map to see where the birds in this book can be found in the wild.

NORTH AMERICA

American robin
American white pelican
Atlantic puffin
bald eagle
barn swallow
blue jay
house sparrow
keel-billed toucan
king vulture
magnificent frigatebird
northern cardinal
peregrine falcon
pileated woodpecker
ruby-throated hummingbird
snowy owl
western grebe
wood duck
wood thrush

SOUTH AMERICA

barn swallow
house sparrow
keel-billed toucan
king vulture
magnificent frigatebird
peregrine falcon
rufous hornero

EUROPE

Atlantic puffin
barn swallow
common cuckoo
house sparrow
peregrine falcon
snowy owl

ASIA

barn swallow
common cuckoo
house sparrow
peregrine falcon
red-crowned crane
snowy owl
Vogelkop bowerbird
Wilson's bird-of-paradise

AFRICA

barn swallow
common cuckoo
house sparrow
ostrich
peregrine falcon
red-billed oxpecker
sociable weaver

AUSTRALIA

Australian brush-turkey
house sparrow
peregrine falcon
rainbow lorikeet
royal penguin (Macquarie Island and southern Pacific Ocean)

PARENT TIPS

Extend your child's experience beyond the pages of this book. Setting up a bird feeder near a window of your house, pointing out birds when you're walking outside with your child, and visiting your local zoo's aviary are great ways to continue satisfying your child's curiosity about birds. Here are some other activities you can do with National Geographic's *Little Kids First Big Book of Birds*.

BIRD CARD GAME

(NUMBERS)

Have your child pick 20 of his favorite birds from this book. Help him draw a picture of each bird on one side of an index card. Number the cards—on the picture side—1 through 20. Shuffle the cards and deal ten to each player. (Add to the number of cards you make if more than two people play.) Each player lays down one card for each turn. Whoever has the card with the higher number gets to keep both cards. The player with the most cards at the end wins.

LISTEN TO BIRD SONGS

(MUSIC)

Ask your child which bird songs she'd like to hear. You can find bird songs online. The National Audubon Society and The Cornell Lab of Ornithology are a couple of sites where you can hear bird songs. Look for birds your child has seen in your neighborhood and play their songs and calls. Ask your child whether she's heard the sounds outside. Encourage her to listen to birds and to try to identify them by their song.

GO BIRDING

(OBSERVATION)

Take your child on an outing specifically to look for birds. Have your child look for birds in the trees and on the ground. If you're near a lake or marsh, watch for water birds. Have your child practice looking through binoculars. When he spots a bird, encourage him to describe what he sees: What color(s) is the bird? How big is it? What shape beak does it have? What is it doing? Use a bird guide to help your child figure out what species of bird he's spotted. Keep a list of all the birds you see. When you get home, reinforce what your child has seen by finding and playing the birds' songs/calls online (see Listen to Bird Songs, left).

CREATE A BIRD POSTER

(ARTS AND CRAFTS)

Provide your child with poster board, crayons, markers, glue sticks, and a variety of materials (such as feathers, sequins, glitter) that you can find at a craft store. Challenge her to create a poster to hang in her room. She might want to draw and decorate a bowerbird's arena, create a bird-of-paradise with all its feather finery, or make a bird guide of her neighborhood species.

RESPLENDENT QUETZAL

STATE BIRDS

(GEOGRAPHY)

Go online to join Barry the Bald Eagle on a state-by-state rap tour of the United States, each one co-hosted by a state bird. Watch with your child as he learns facts about each state, as described by animated birds in this series of animated rap music videos that will have you and your child singing along.

kids.nationalgeographic.com/videos/50-birds-50-states

BIRD JOKES

(HUMOR)

Goofy jokes lead to fun, giggles, laughter, and silly word play. Find bird jokes online or in joke books, or make up your own. Encourage your child to make up a few, too. Here are three to get you started:

Q: Why do hummingbirds hum?
A: Because they forgot the words!

Q: What does a duck like to eat with soup?
A: Quackers!

Q: What bird is with you at every meal?
A: A swallow!

GLOSSARY

RED-AND-GREEN MACAW

ALTRICIAL
chicks that are helpless (require parents to care for and feed them) and undeveloped (eyes closed and few, if any, feathers) when they hatch

BINOCULARS
a device with eyepieces for each eye to look through that makes distant things look closer, allowing the user to see more detail

FLEDGE
the point at which a chick has grown the muscles and feathers it needs to survive with little or no help from its parent(s)

FLOCK
a group of the same kind of bird that is feeding, resting, or traveling together

INCUBATE
keeping eggs safe and warm until they hatch

PRECOCIAL
chicks that are able to leave the nest soon after hatching and feed themselves; precocial chicks hatch quite fully developed

PREDATOR
an animal that hunts other animals (prey) for food

PREY
an animal that a predator hunts and kills for food

SCAVENGER
an animal that finds and eats dead animals that it didn't kill itself

SPECIES
a category, or kind, of unique animal or plant

STOOP
a bird's fast dive down through the air as it hunts its prey

CREDITS

Front cover: Dave Watts/Nature Picture Library; **Spine:** OlegDoroshin/Shutterstock; **Back cover:** (UP), Bill Coster/Ardea; (LO), Steve Byland/Shutterstock; 1, Tim Zurowski/BIA/Minden Pictures; 2-3, Jan Vermeer/Minden Pictures; 4 (LE), Joseph Gough/Dreamstime; 4 (RT), Dpullman/Dreamstime; 5 (UP), Louis-Marie Preau/Nature Picture Library; 5 (LO), Bonnie Taylor Barry/Shutterstock; 8-9, duangnapa_b/Shutterstock; 10 (LE), Panuruangjan/Dreamstime; 10 (RT), Potapov Alexander/Shutterstock; 11 (UP), Brian Kushner/Dreamstime; 11 (LO LE), George Robertson/Dreamstime; 11 (LO CTR), Edwin Kats/NIS/Minden Pictures; 11 (LO RT), FloridaStock/Shutterstock; 12, Super Prin/Shutterstock; 13 (UP), Emilio100/Shutterstock; 13 (LO), Sergey Gorshkov/Minden Pictures; 14 (LE), blickwinkel/Alamy; 15 (UP RT), Anthony Mercieca/Science Source; 15 (CTR LE), Markus Varesvuo/Minden Pictures; 15 (LO), Hakoar/Dreamstime; 16 (UP), Feng Yu/Shutterstock; 16 (LO LE), Vishnevskiy Vasily/Shutterstock; 16 (LO RT), Vishnevskiy Vasily/Shutterstock; 17 (LE), Steve Byland/Dreamstime; 17 (UP), bofotolux/Shutterstock; 17 (UP CTR), Cuson/Shutterstock; 17 (LO CTR), Vitaly Ilyasov/Shutterstock; 17 (LO), Torikell/Dreamstime; 18-19, Klein & Hubert/Nature Picture Library; 20 (CTR), iStockphoto/Getty Images; 20 (LE), Shutterstock; 21, Willism Osborn/Nature Picture Library; 22 (LE), Ralph Lee Hopkins/National Geographic Creative; 22 (RT), Shutterstock; 23 (UP), Sam Hobson/Nature Picture Library; 23 (LO), imageBROKER/Alamy; 24 (CTR), Steve Maslowski/Visuals Unlimited, Inc./Getty Images; 24 (RT), Shutterstock; 25, Asif Islam/Shutterstock; 26 (CTR LE), JNB Photography/Shutterstock; 26 (UP RT), Michael & Patricia Fogden/Minden Pictures; 26 (LO LE), Tom Vezo/Minden Pictures; 26 (LO RT), Ondrej Prosicky/Shutterstock; 27 (UP LE), Frans Lanting/National Geographic Creative; 27 (UP RT), Michael & Patricia Fogden/Minden Pictures/National Geographic Creative; 27 (LO LE), Glenn Bartley/BIA/Minden Pictures; 27 (LO RT), Tom Vezo/Minden Pictures; 28, Klein & Hubert/Nature Picture Library; 29 (LE), Ingo Arndt/Minden Pictures; 29 (LO RT), Eric Baccega/Nature Picture Library; 29 (CTR RT), Shutterstock; 29 (CTR RT), Shutterstock; 30 (UP), Richard Du Toit/Getty Images; 30 (LO LE), Eliot Lyons/Minden Pictures; 30 (LO RT), Frans Lanting/National Geographic Creative; 31 (UP LE), Meister Photos/Shutterstock; 31 (UP RT), Awcnz62/Dreamstime; 31 (LO LE), Cyril Ruoso/Minden Pictures; 31 (LO RT), Luciano Candisani/Minden Pictures; 32 (CTR), Otto Plantema/Buiten-beeld/Minden Pictures; 32 (LO RT), Shutterstock; 32 (LO RT), Shutterstock; 33 (UP), Ole Jorgen Liodden/NPL/Minden Pictures; 33 (LO), Daniel A. Bedell/National Geographic Creative; 34 (UP), Alex Mustard/2020 Vision/Minden Pictures; 34 (LO), Michael Robbins/Dreamstime; 35 (CTR), Leksele/Shutterstock; 35 (LO LE), Shutterstock; 36 (UP), Russell Watkins/Shutterstock; 36 (LO), Michael Robbins/Dreamstime; 37, Mark Caunt/Shutterstock; 38 (UP LE), Joel Sartore/National Geographic Creative; 38 (LO LE), S & D & K Maslowski/Minden Pictures; 38 (RT), Joseph Gough/Dreamstime; 39 (UP LE), Frans Lanting/National Geographic Creative; 39 (CTR LE), Kristoffbakkes/Dreamstime; 39 (UP RT), Konrad Wothe/Minden Pictures/National Geographic Creative; 39 (LO LE), Lukas Blazek/Dreamstime; 39 (LO RT), Chris Hill/Dreamstime; 40-41, Toshiaki Ida/Nature Production/Minden Pictures; 42 (UP LE), Tom Vezo/Minden Pictures/National Geographic Creative; 42 (LO LE), Wavebreakmedia Ltd./Dreamstime; 42 (RT), Dreamstime; 43, S & D & K Maslowski/Minden Pictures; 44 (CTR), Pictureguy66/Dreamstime; 44 (LO LE), Shutterstock; 44 (LO LE), Donald M. Jones/Minden Pictures; 45, Verdon Tomajko; 46, Ron Dudley; 47 (UP), Jim Brandenburg/Minden Pictures; 47 (LO), Robert Harding/Alamy; 48, Shutterstock; 48, Shutterstock; 49, Mikelane45/Dreamstime; 50, 2/Anna Henly/Ocean/Corbis; 51, Gerrit Vyn/Minden Pictures; 52, Nataliya Taratunina/Dreamstime; 53, Prisma Bildagentur AG/Alamy; 53 (LE), Shutterstock; 54, Konrad Wothe/Minden Pictures; 54 (LO RT), Shutterstock; 55, Otto Plantema/Buiten-beeld/Minden Pictures; 56 (UP RT), Tim Laman/National Geographic Creative; 56 (UP LE), Tim Laman/National Geographic Creative; 56 (LO LO), Tim Laman/National Geographic Creative; 56 (LO RT), Tim Laman/National Geographic Creative; 57 (UP LE), Tim Laman/Nature Picture Library; 57 (UP RT), Tim Laman/National Geographic Creative; 57 (CTR LE), Tim Laman/National Geographic Creative; 57 (LO LE), Tim Laman/National Geographic Creative; 57 (LO RT), Tim Laman/National Geographic Creative; 58 (LO2), Andre Gilden/NIS/Minden Pictures; 58 (UP3), George Grall/National Geographic Creative; 58 (UP2), Steve Gettle/Minden Pictures; 58 (UP1), Mikelane45/Dreamstime; 58 (UP4), Mikelane45/Dreamstime; 58 (LO5), Konrad Wothe/Minden Pictures; 58 (LO1), Konrad Wothe/Minden Pictures; 58 (LO4), Nataliya Taratunina/Dreamstime; 58 (UP4), Steve Gettle/Minden Pictures; 59 (UP2), Marciparavia/Dreamstime; 59 (UP1), S & D & K Maslowski/Minden Pictures; 59 (UP3), S & D & K Maslowski/Minden Pictures; 59 (CTR2), Mikelane45/Dreamstime; 59 (LO2), Konrad Wothe/Minden Pictures; 59 (LO4), Konrad Wothe/Minden Pictures; 59 (LO3), Nataliya Taratunina/Dreamstime; 59 (UP4), Marciparavia/Dreamstime; 59 (LO1), Andre Gilden/NIS/Minden Pictures; 59 (CTR3), Steve Gettle/Minden Pictures; 59 (CTR4), George Grall/National Geographic Creative; 59 (CTR1), George Grall/National Geographic Creative; 60-61, Heike Odermatt/Minden Pictures; 62, Alan Murphy/BIA/Minden Pictures; 62 (LO RT), Shutterstock; 63, Tom Vezo/Minden Pictures/National Geographic Creative; 64 (UP), Mircea Costina/Dreamstime; 64 (LO), George Grall/National Geographic Creative; 65, Jesse Nguyen/Shutterstock; 66, Rob Christiaans/Dreamstime; 66 (LE), Shutterstock; 67 (UP), Papilio/Alamy; 67 (LO), Ijdema/Dreamstime; 68, Ann and Steve Toon/Alamy; 69, Alexander Koenders/NiS/Minden Pictures; 69 (RT), Shutterstock; 70 (UP), Michael Fritzen/Alamy; 70 (LO), Ralf Broskvar/Dreamstime; 70, Dreamstime; 71, Juan-Carlos Munoz/Minden Pictures; 72, Konrad Wothe/Minden Pictures/National Geographic Creative; 72 (RT), Barrie Britton/Minden Pictures; 73, Tim Laman/Nature Picture Library; 74 (UP), Ingo Arndt/Nature Picture Library; 74 (UP CTR), Richard Kirby/Nature Picture Library; 74 (LO CTR), Ingo Arndt/Nature Picture Library; 74 (LO), Tim Laman/Nature Picture Library; 75, Konrad Wothe/Minden Pictures; 76, Kim Taylor/Nature Picture Library; 77, Steve Gettle/Minden Pictures; 77 (LO LE), Shutterstock; 78 (LE), George Grall/National Geographic Creative; 78 (RT), Steve Gettle/Minden Pictures; 79, Steve Gettle/Minden Pictures; 79 (LO RT), Shutterstock; 80, Scott Leslie/Minden Pictures; 81 (UP), Stan Tekiela; 81 (LO), S & D & K Maslowski/Minden Pictures; 82, Don Pitcher/National Geographic Creative; 83 (UP), Paul Nicklen/National Geographic Creative; 83 (LO), Suzi Eszterhas/Minden Pictures; 83 (LO LE), Shutterstock; 83 (LO LE), Shutterstock; 84, William Osborn/NPL/Minden Pictures; 84 (LE), Dreamstime; 84 (LE), Shutterstock; 85, D. Parer & E. Parer-Cook/Minden Pictures; 86, D. Parer & E. Parer-Cook/Minden Pictures; 87, D. Parer & E. Parer-Cook/Minden Pictures; 88, Toshiyuki Yoshino/Nature Production/Minden Pictures; 89 (UP), Wolfgang Brandmeier/BIA/Minden Pictures; 89 (LO), tobkatrina/Shutterstock; 89 (LO LE), Shutterstock; 90 (UP LE), Martin Woike/FN/Minden Pictures/National Geographic Creative; 90 (LO LE), Luiz Claudio Marigo/Nature Picture Library; 90 (CTR), Ann and Steve Toon/Alamy; 91 (UP), Luiz Claudio Marigo/Nature Picture Library; 91 (CTR), Ingo Arndt/Minden Pictures; 91 (LO), Cyril Ruoso/Minden Pictures; 92-93, John Waters/Nature Picture Library; 94, Claudio Contreras/Nature Picture Library; 94 (LO LE), Shutterstock; 94 (LO LE), Shutterstock; 95, Tze-hsin Woo/Getty Images; 96, Martin Withers/FLPA/Minden Pictures; 97 (UP), Lynn M. Stone/Nature Picture Library; 97 (LO), Paul Reeves Photography/Shutterstock; 98, Photographer/Nature Picture Library; 98 (LE), Shutterstock; 98 (LE), Shutterstock; 99, All Canada Photos/Alamy; 100-101 (UP), Alan Murphy/BIA/Minden Pictures; 100 (LO LE), Ingo Waschkies/BIA/Minden Pictures; 100 (LO RT), Tania Thomson/Shutterstock; 101 (LE), David M. Dennis/Animals Animals/Earth Scenes/National Geographic Creative; 101 (RT), Kim Taylor/NPL/Minden Pictures; 102 (LE), SuperStock/Alamy; 103, Jiri Slama/BIA/Minden Pictures; 103 (RT), Dreamstime; 103 (RT), Shutterstock; 104, Mykhaylo Lytvynyuk/National Geographic Creative; 105 (UP), Steve Maslowski/Visuals Unlimited; 105 (CTR), Paul Rommer/Shutterstock; 105 (RT), George Grall/National Geographic Creative; 106, Marie Read/NPL/Minden Pictures; 107, Donald M. Jones/Minden Pictures; 107 (LO LE), Shutterstock; 108, Marie Read/Nature Picture Library; 108 (LE), Shutterstock; 109 (UP), Alan Murphy/BIA/Minden Pictures; 109 (LO), Dionisvera/Shutterstock; 110, Heini Wehrle/BIA/Minden Pictures; 110 (RT), Shutterstock; 111 (RT), Richard Du Toit/Minden Pictures/National Geographic Creative; 111 (CTR), Piotr Naskrecki/Minden Pictures; 112, Tim Fitzharris/Minden Pictures; 113, Gregory Basco/Visuals Unlimited, Inc.; 113 (LO LE), Shutterstock; 113 (LO LE), Shutterstock; 114, Suzi Eszterhas/Minden Pictures; 115 (UP), Jim Crosswell; 115 (LO), Suzi Eszterhas/Minden Pictures; 116 (LE), Jason Edwards/National Geographic Creative; 116 (RT), Roy Toft/National Geographic Creative; 117, Pete Oxford/Minden Pictures/National Geographic Creative; 117 (LO LE), Dreamstime; 117 (LO LE), Shutterstock;118 (UP LE), Lynn M. Stone/Nature Picture Library; 118 (LO LE), All Canada Photos/Alamy; 118 (RT), Rich Reid/National Geographic Creative; 119 (UP CTR), Tui De Roy/Minden Pictures/National Geographic Creative; 119 (CTR LE), George Grall/National Geographic Creative; 119 (LO LE), James Pierce/Shutterstock; 119 (UP RT), Christophe Courteau/Nature Picture Library; 119 (LO RT), Frans Lanting/National Geographic Creative; 123, Juan Carlos Vindas/NIS/Minden Pictures; 124, Pete Oxford/Minden Pictures; 128, Alan Murphy/BIA/Minden Pictures

INDEX

For Dad —C.D.H.

A special thank-you to Jonathan Alderfer, author, illustrator, and National Geographic's bird expert, whose time and expertise were invaluable in the preparation of this book.

Since 1888, the National Geographic Society has funded more than 12,000 research, exploration, and preservation projects around the world. The Society receives funds from National Geographic Partners LLC, funded in part by your purchase. A portion of the proceeds from this book supports this vital work. To learn more, visit www.natgeo.com/info.

For more information, visit www.nationalgeographic.com, call 1-800-647-5463, or write to the following address:
National Geographic Partners, LLC
1145 17th Street N.W.
Washington, D.C. 20036-4688 U.S.A.

Visit us online at nationalgeographic.com/books

For librarians and teachers: ngchildrensbooks.org

More for kids from National Geographic: kids.nationalgeographic.com

For information about special discounts for bulk purchases, please contact National Geographic Books Special Sales: specialsales@natgeo.com

For rights or permissions inquiries, please contact National Geographic Books Subsidiary Rights: bookrights@natgeo.com

NATIONAL GEOGRAPHIC and Yellow Border Design are trademarks of the National Geographic Society, used under license.

Art Directed by Amanda Larsen
Designed by Amber Colleran

Trade hardcover ISBN: 978-1-4263-2432-1
Reinforced library edition ISBN: 978-1-4263-2433-8

Printed in China
17/PPS/1 BX

BLUE JAY

MARK RIETVELD

Voor Mark

x J

EXCEPTIONNEL

BEZET
OCCUPE
ik luister naar
Radio Centraal
wanneer ik wil!
106.7 FM

TAPTONIC

PUCH
LADEN EN LOSSEN
TOEGESTAAN OP
MAANDAG T/M VRIJDAG
VAN 7-11 U. EN 17-19 U.
OP ZATERDAG
VAN 9-11 U. EN 17-18 U.
OP KOOPAVONDEN
VAN 17-19 U. 21-22 U.
Prenten & lijsten
Prenten & lijsten

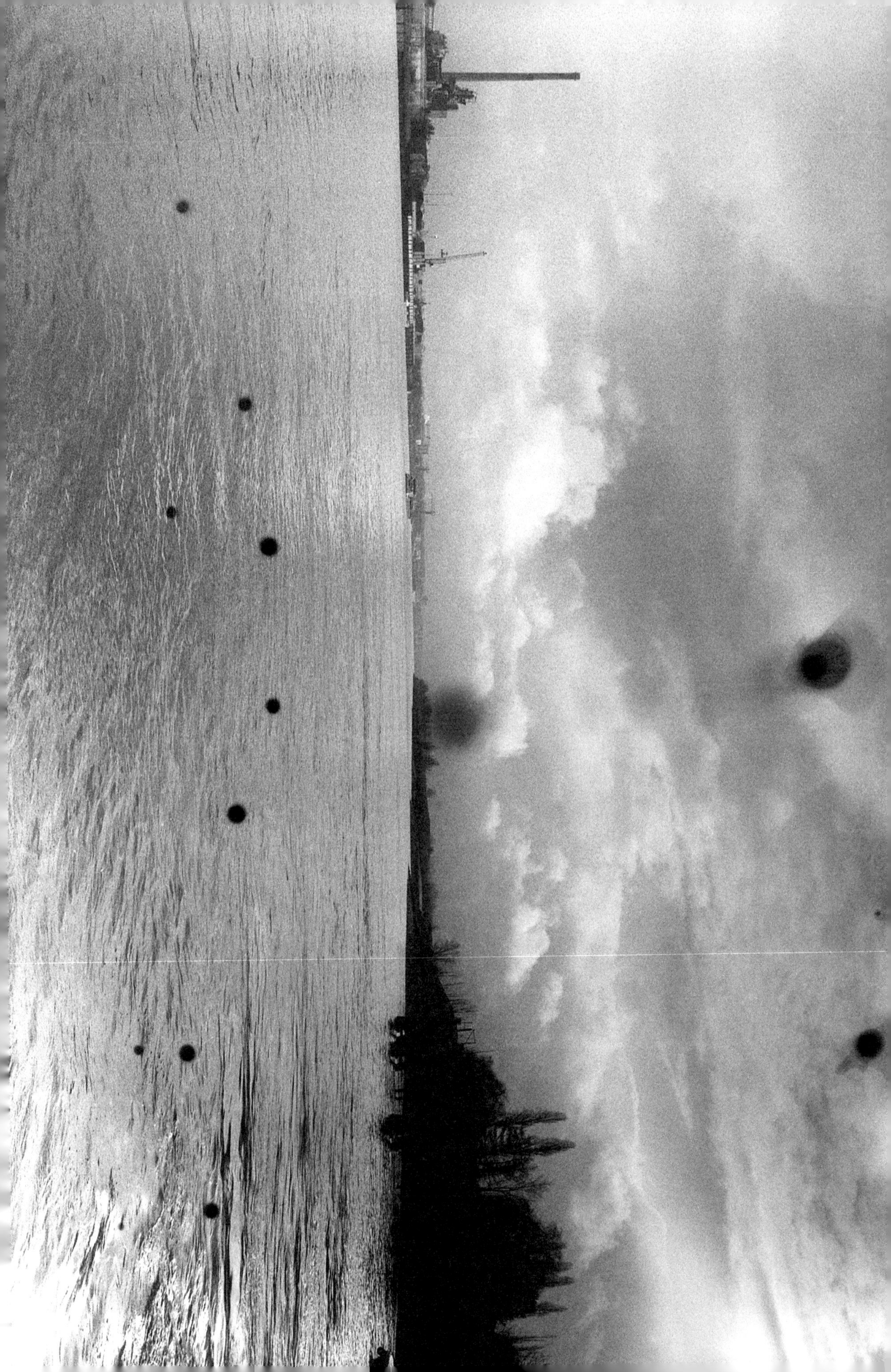

202

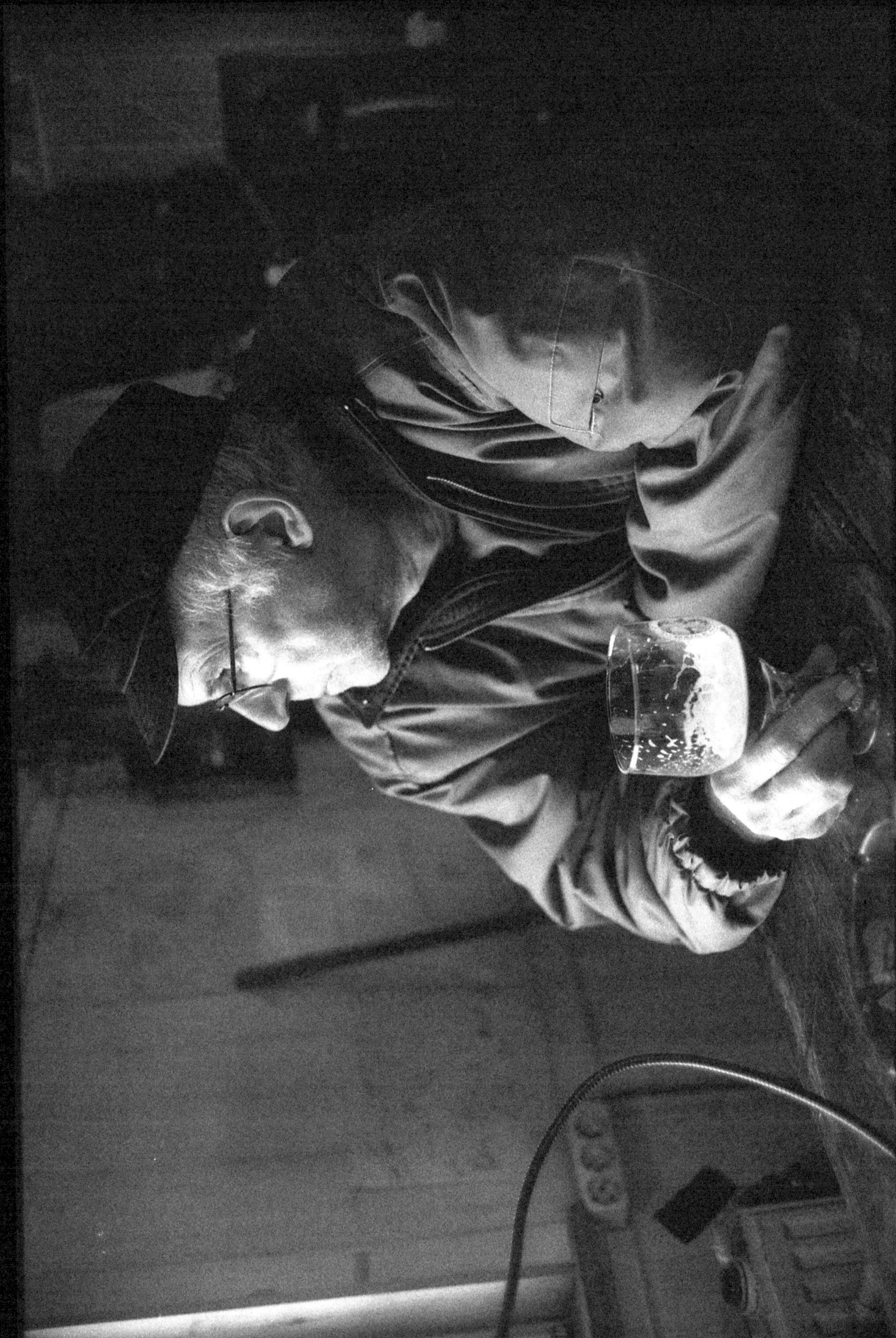

TONIGHT
DSR LINES
LP PRESENTAT
ION!
DJ

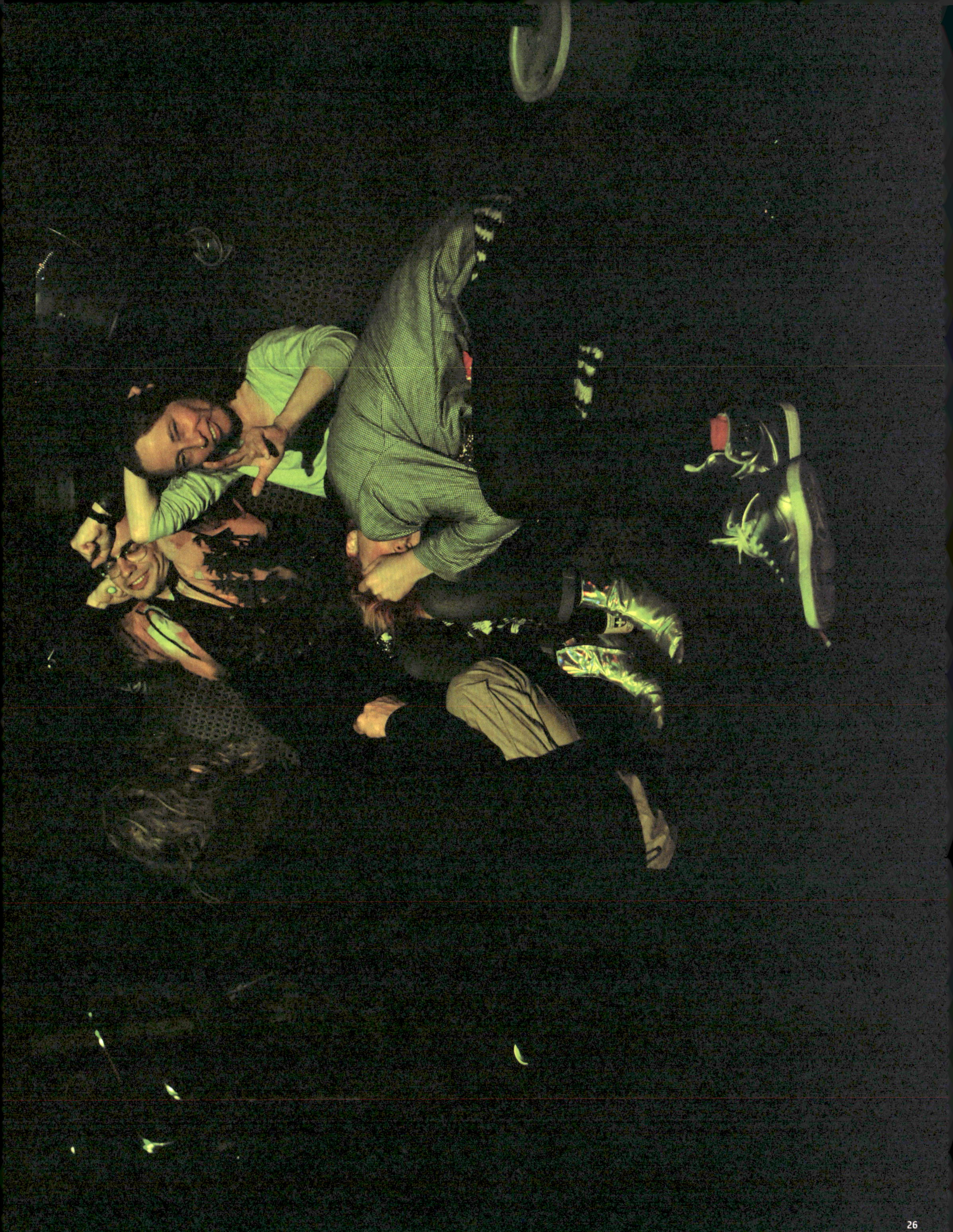

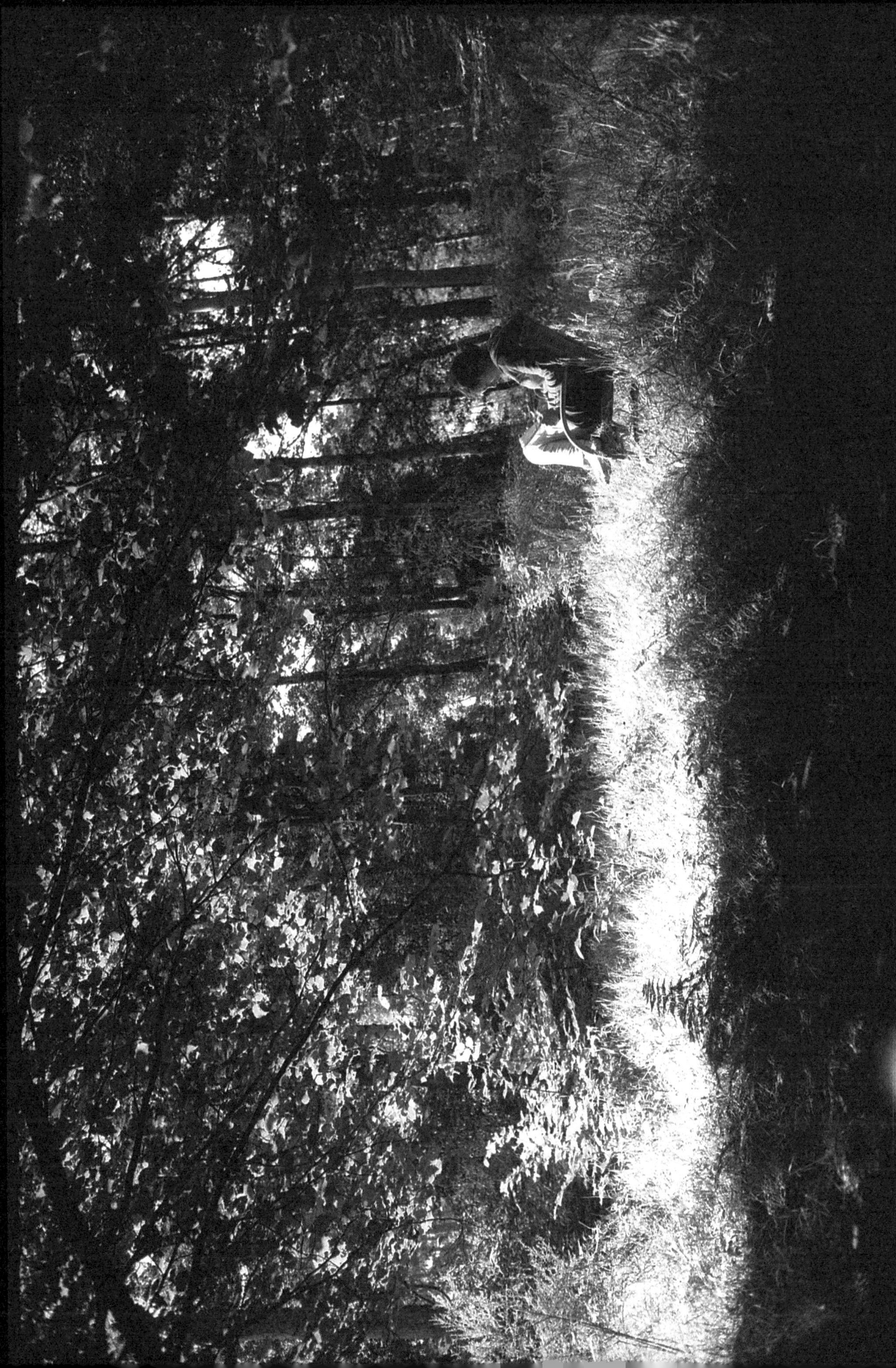

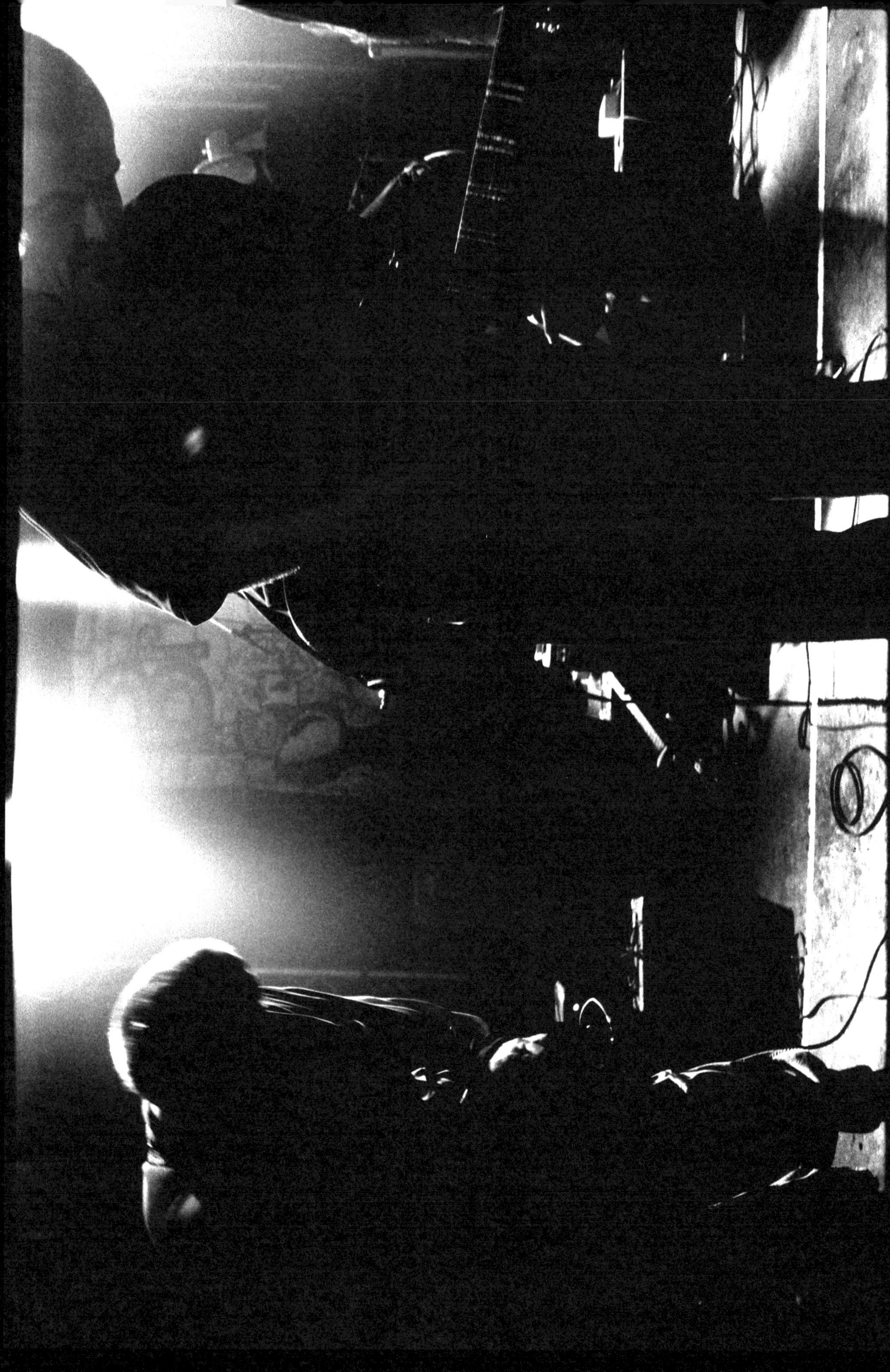

Glaces
Simple Cornet
double Cornet 10.00
Fraise, Vanille ou
Vanille fraise
TIV-TO
LA PULPE D'ORANGE

DJEEM-TRANS
AUTOPRAONICA
ZAMJENA ULJA I FILTERA
VULKANIZER
AUTO DIJELOVI
KOTROMANIĆA 3
TEL. 668-088
MINE!
MINE!
MINE!
MINE!

Všebaráčnická Rychta
23

XA-15-19

STELLA·ARTOIS
VERSE SOEP MET BROOD € 4,00
VERGUNNING STERKE DRANK

VRIJ.
THE NOZEMS
DJ CIZ
21 UUR
10 GLD
EFFENAAR
Vertes

IMPERIAL DECO

BNR
666
GXV
649

Pacifica
YAMAHA

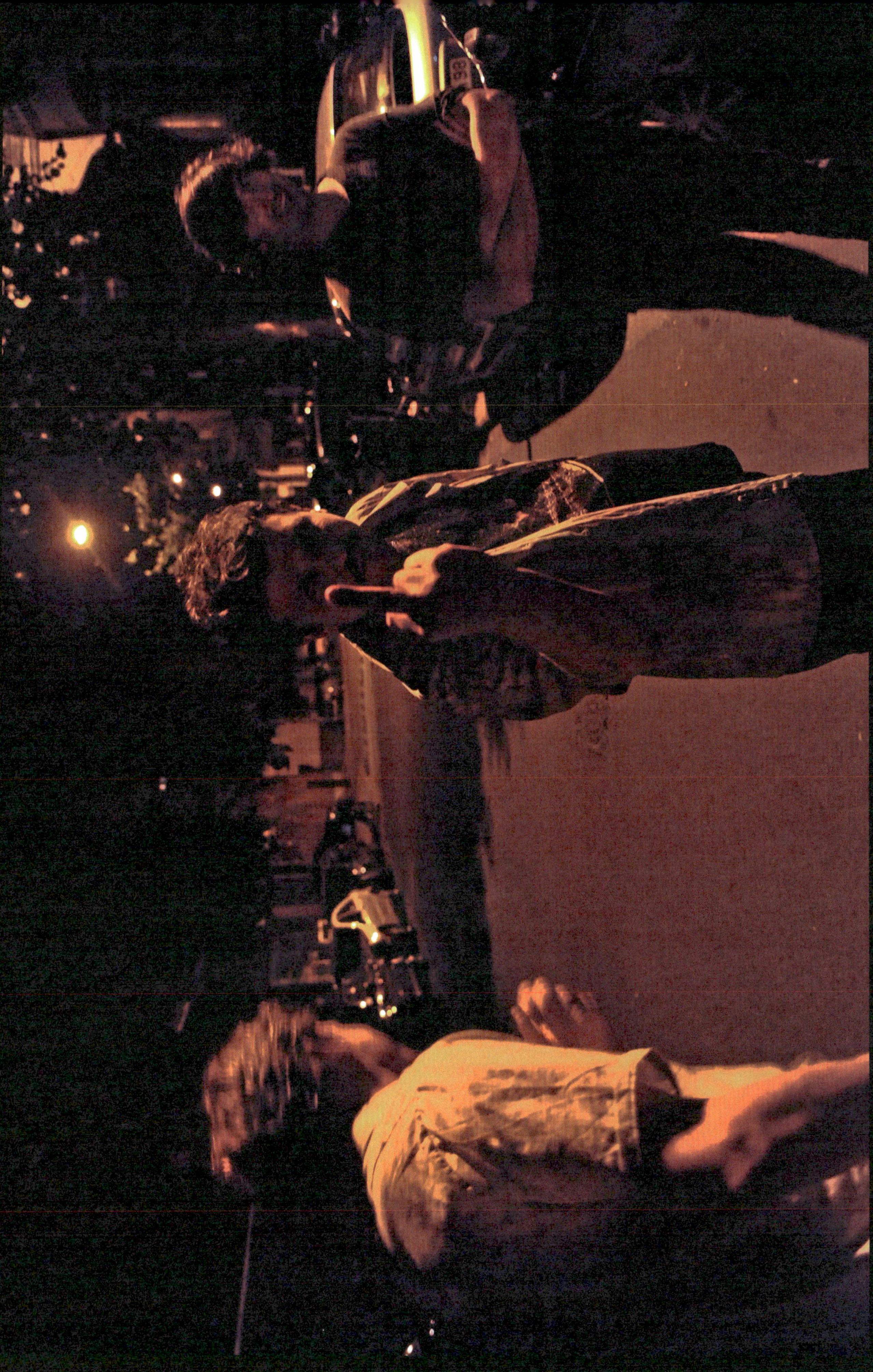

JBL

26

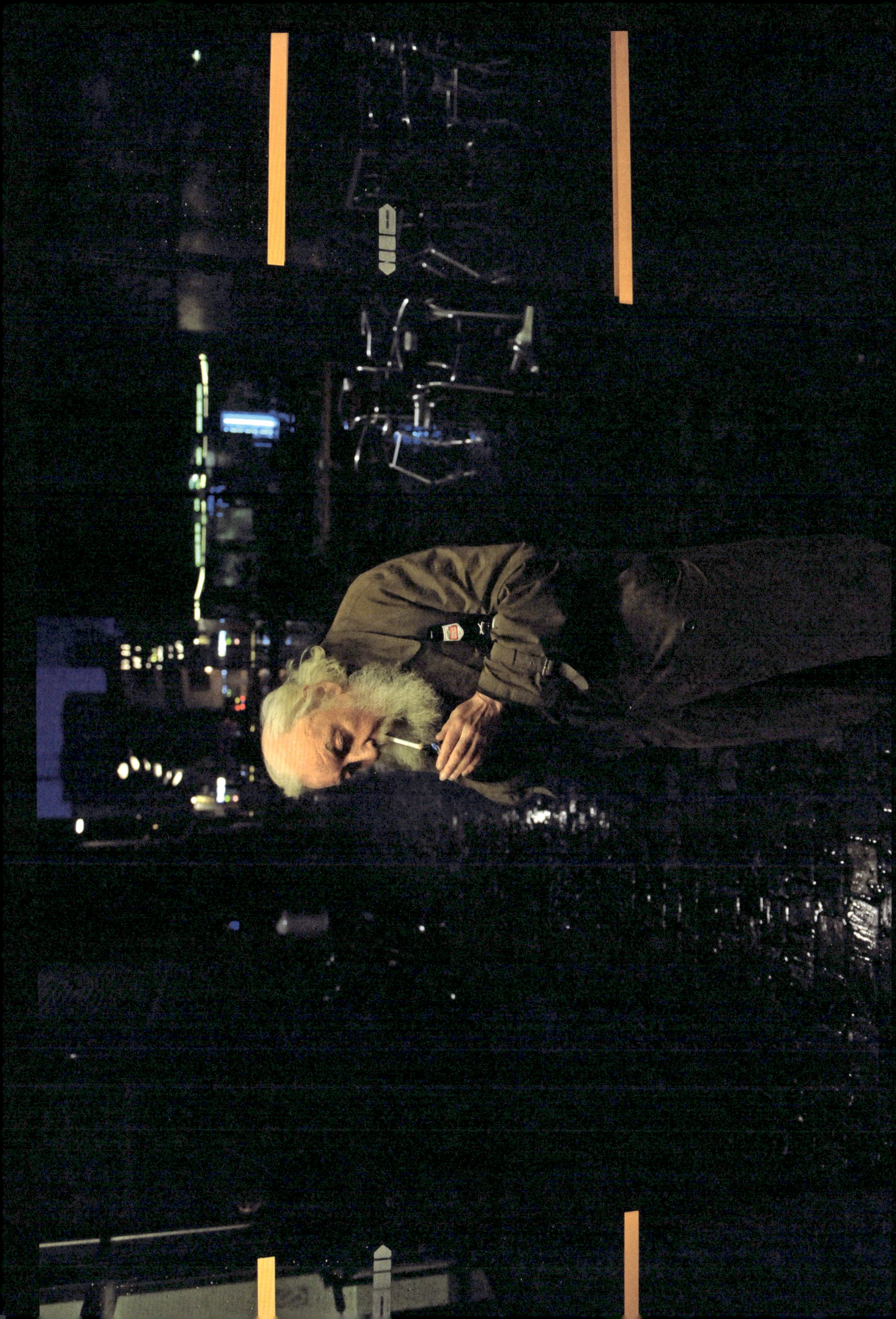

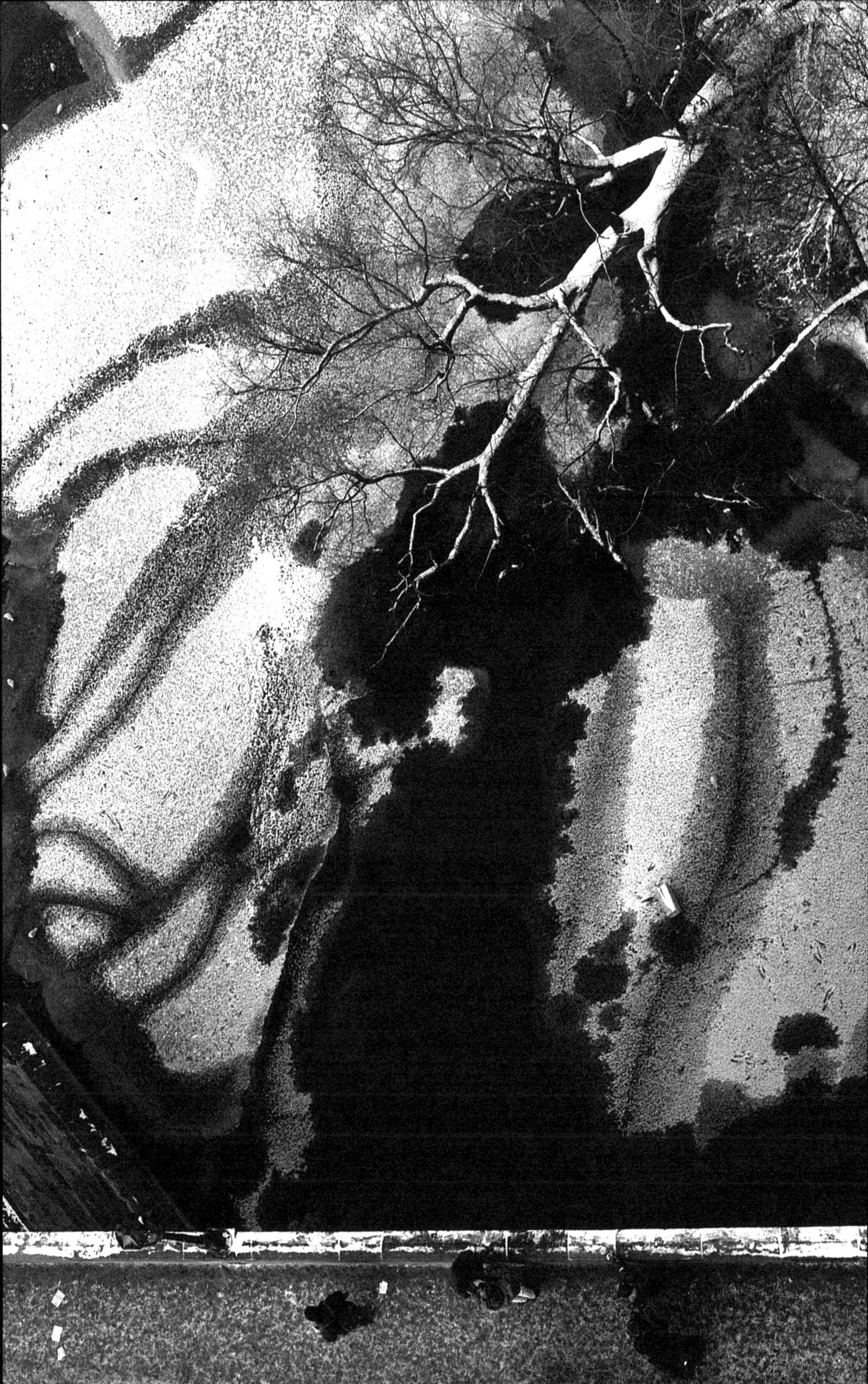

17

STEL ONZE KOFFIE
WWW.CORDONCOFFEE.BE
BOSBAR
OFFIEBRANDERIJ & CAFE
LUNCH
COFFEE
DANSEN
HET BOS
5-6-7 OKTOBER
~DELTA WAVE~
FESTIVAL
BOS
LABS
OKTOB
BOSBAR
OPEN

NOBODY

Peace!

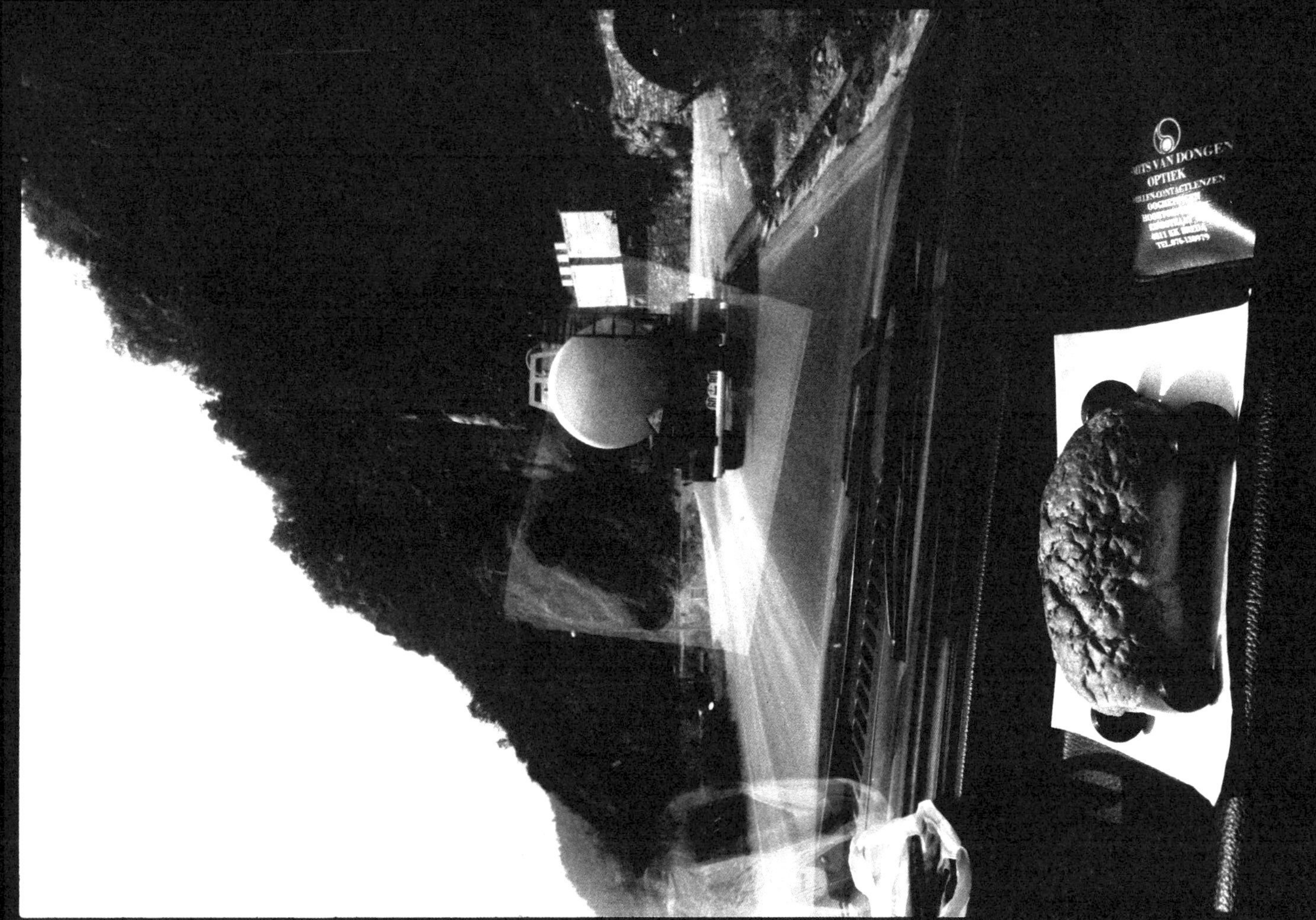
VAN DONGEN
OPTIEK

PUCH

Jupiler

Fender MUSICMASTER

SOCIALE
OCCUPATO
ASCOLTA
RADIO

MSS MEESTERD
PETANQUE
ZONDAG 26/8 OM 2UUR!

EURYBIA
elga
WIN VOOR
500.000 F
CHAMPAGNE
1001
SCHITTERENDE
FEEST
IDEEN
PLAATS VOOR
SCHOLEN EN GROEPEN
PLACE POUR DES
ÈCOLES ET DES GROUPES
PLATZ FÜR SCHULE
UND GRUPPE
DE KONINCK
1833
ATLAS
Kriek. Het geheim van Belle-Vue.

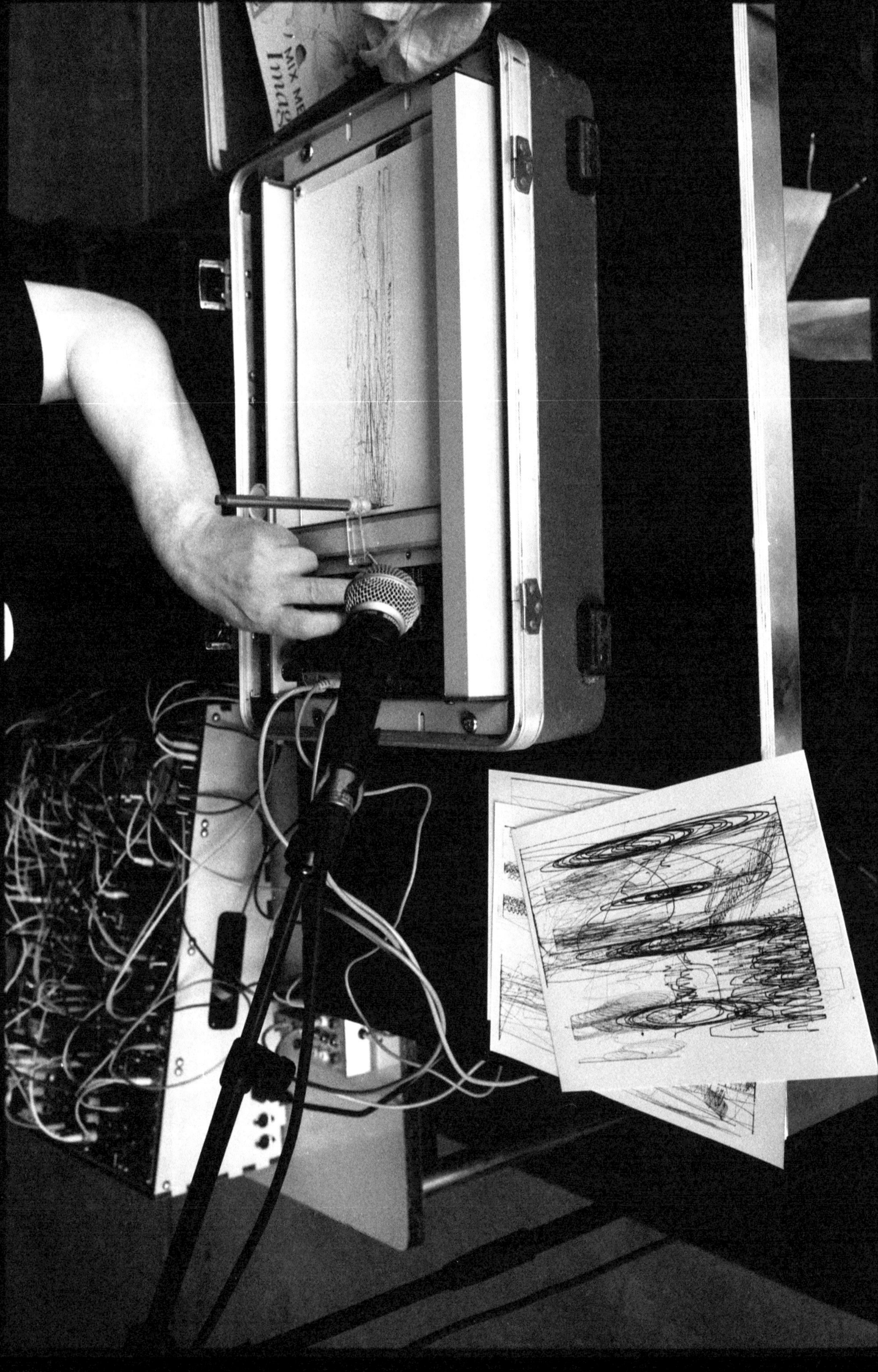

SCHMIDT

dio
centraal
NOVANEX

HEERLIJKE
VIETNAMESE
LOEMPIA'S
OM TE SMULLEN

TENACE

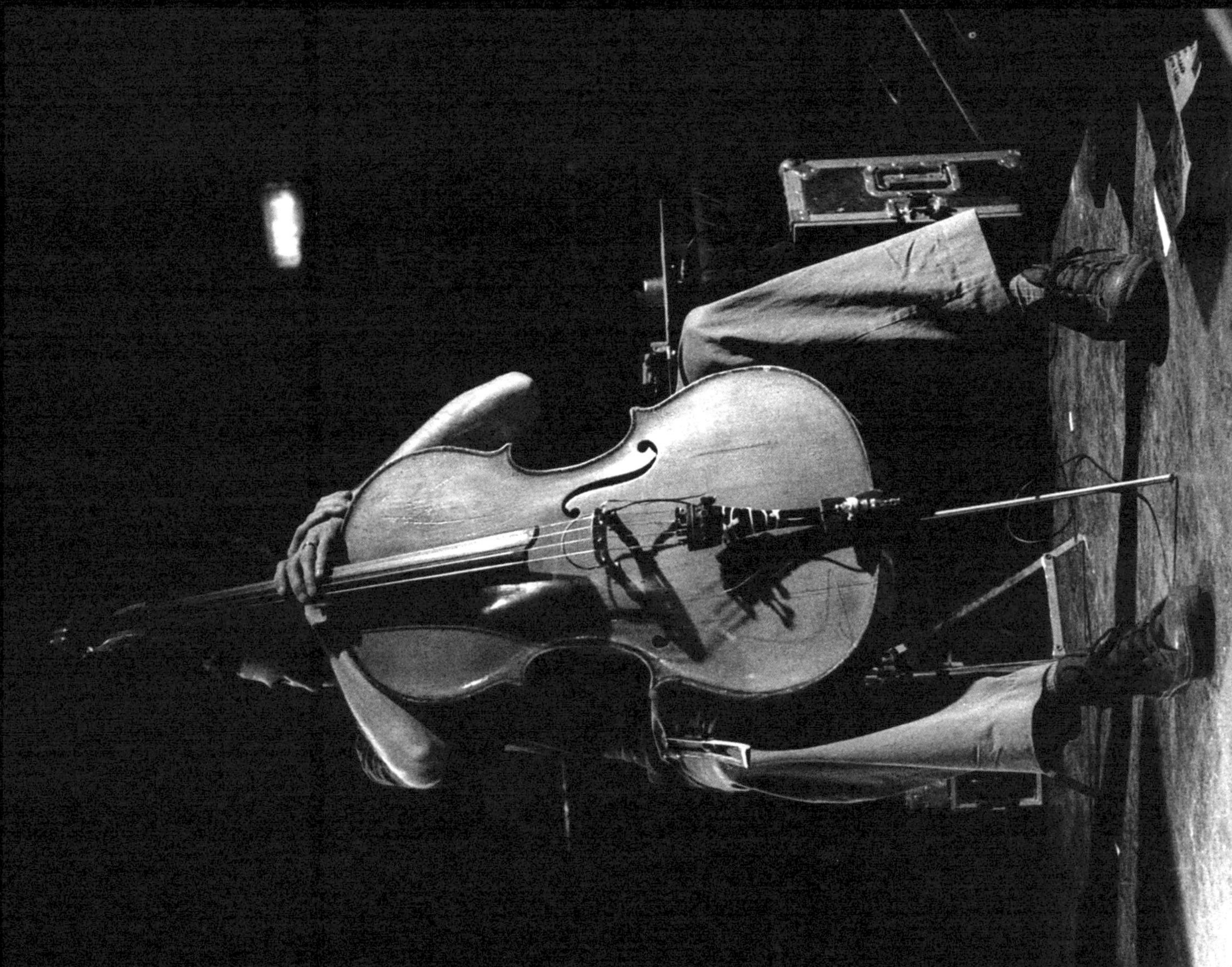

Delifrance®
Meir 26

VLAAMSEOPERA.BE
ZAAL STUURBOORD ANTWERPEN
IN DE CHEMIE
IS ER VOOR ELK
WAT WERK!
SCHRIJF JE GRATIS IN OP
www.wearechemistry.be
WE
ARE
CHEMISTRY

2
ZR 181-14

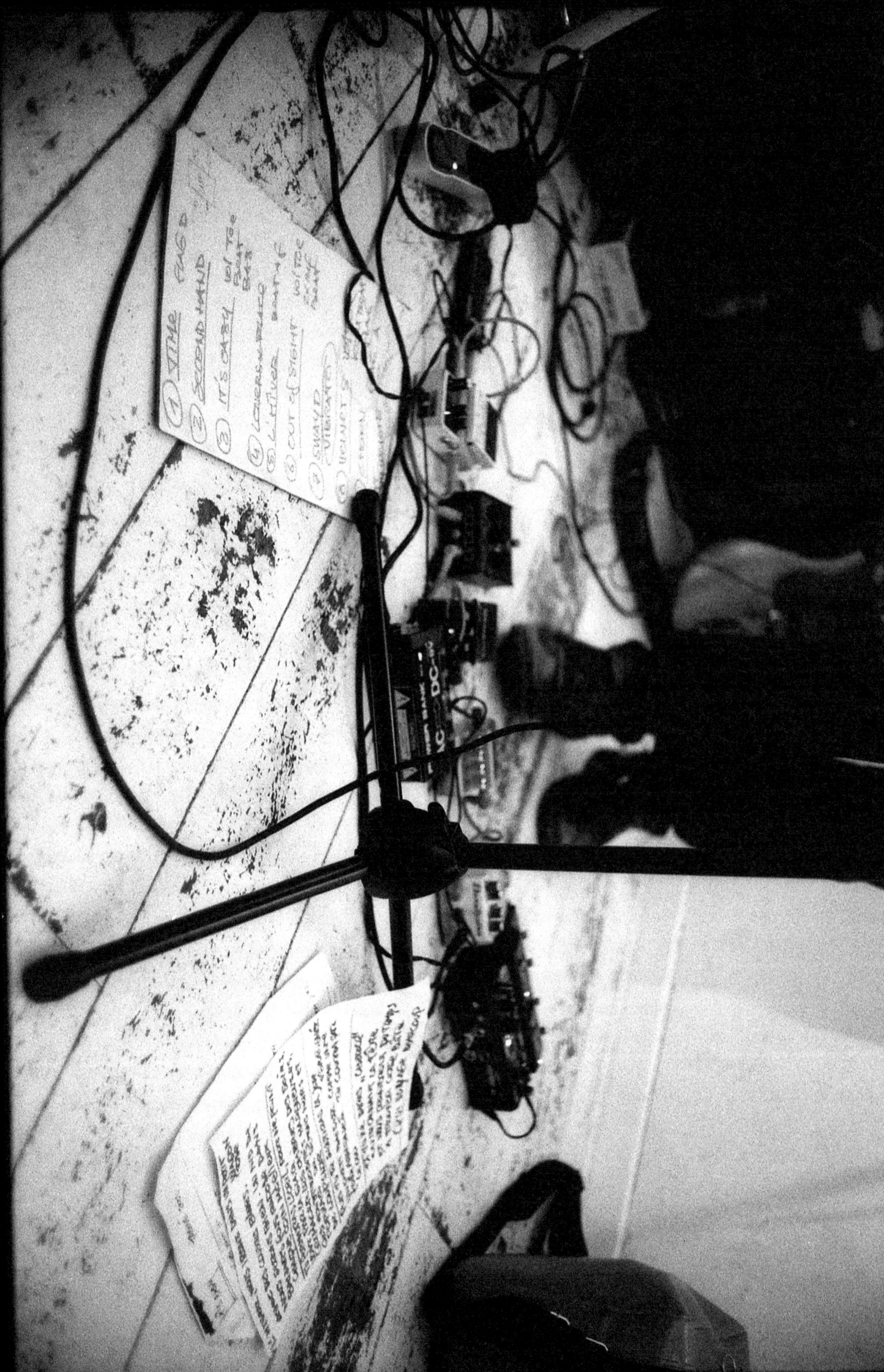

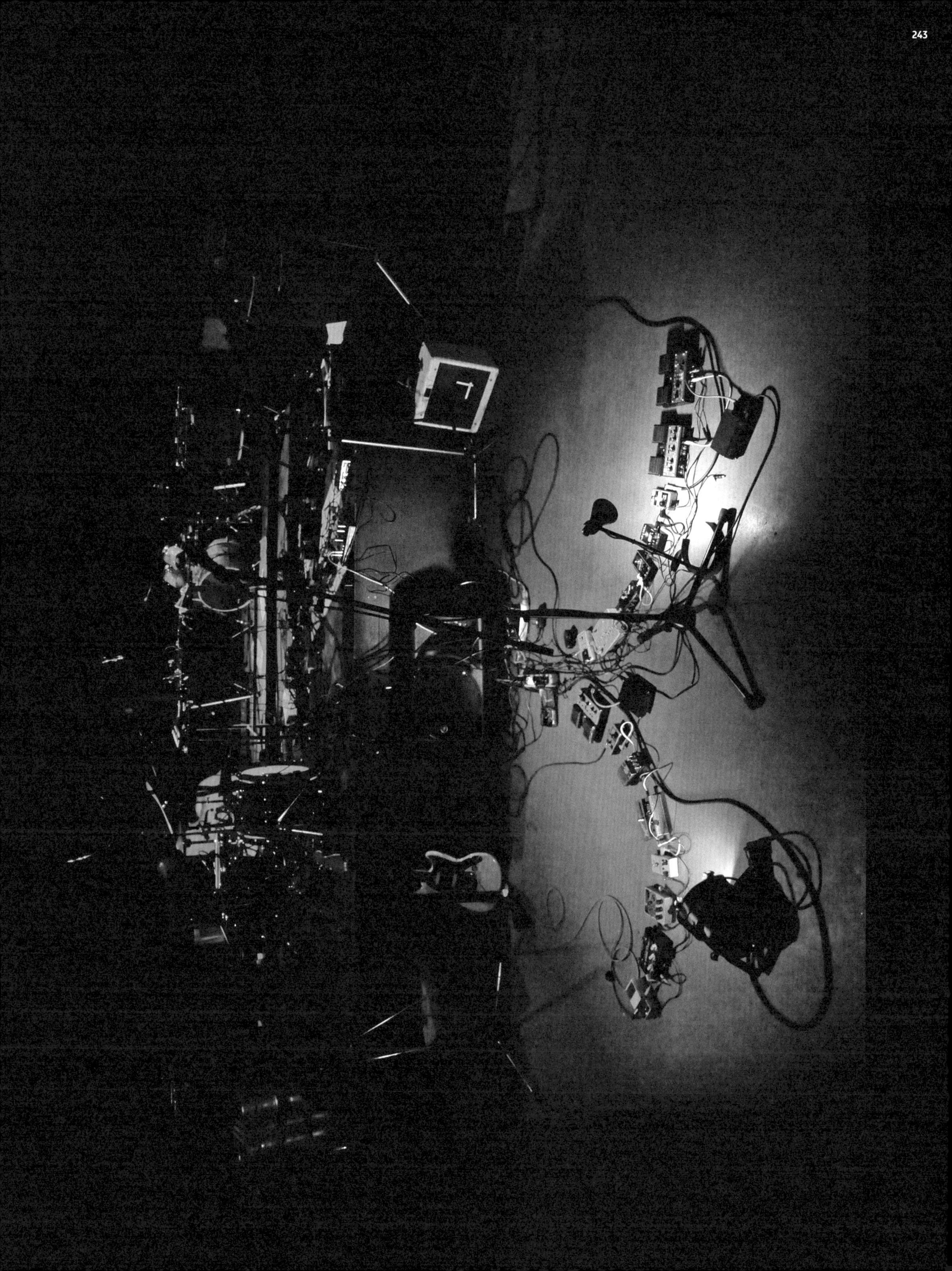

A

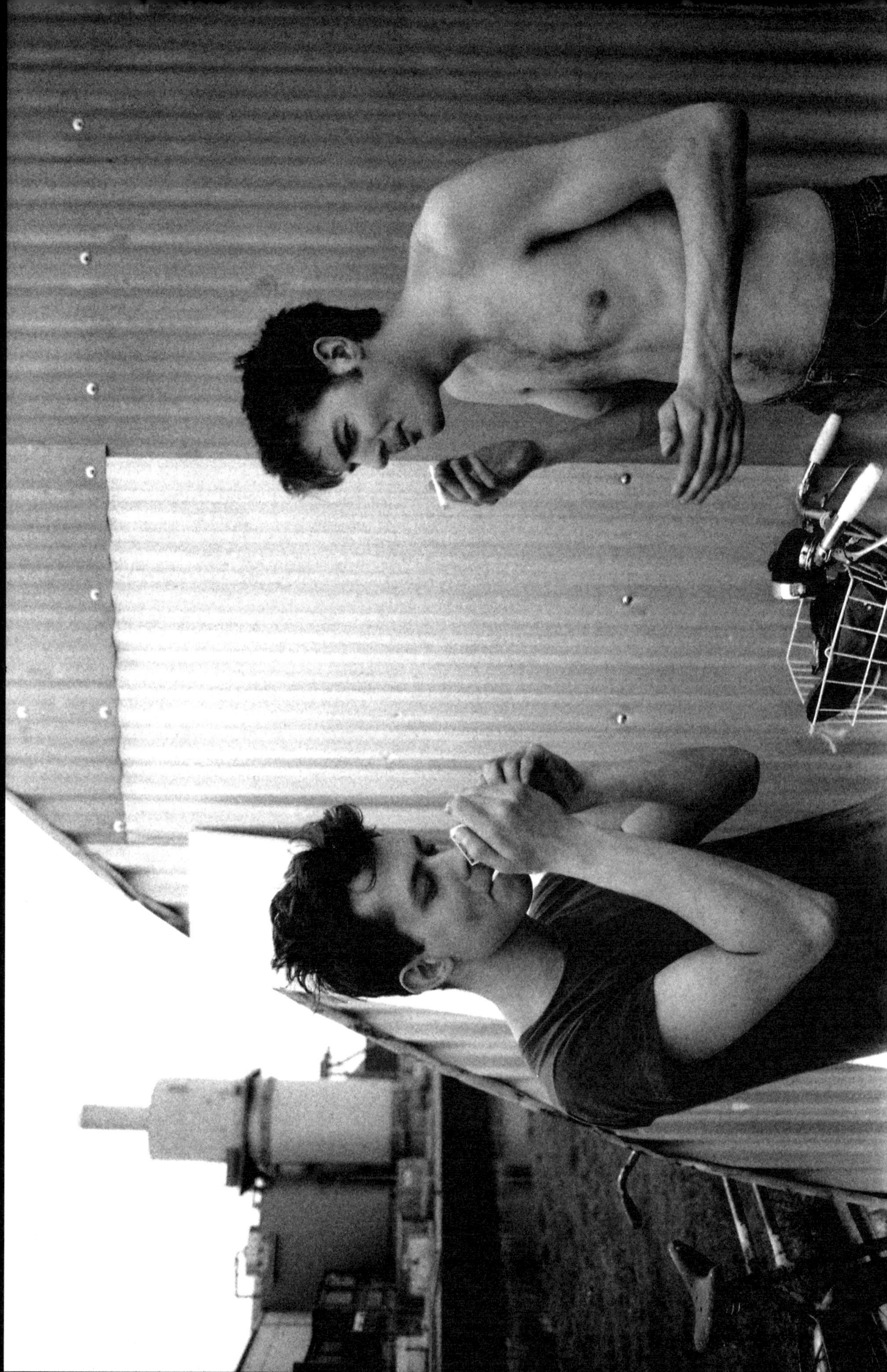

RECEPTION

KRIEK

MAN
DIESEL

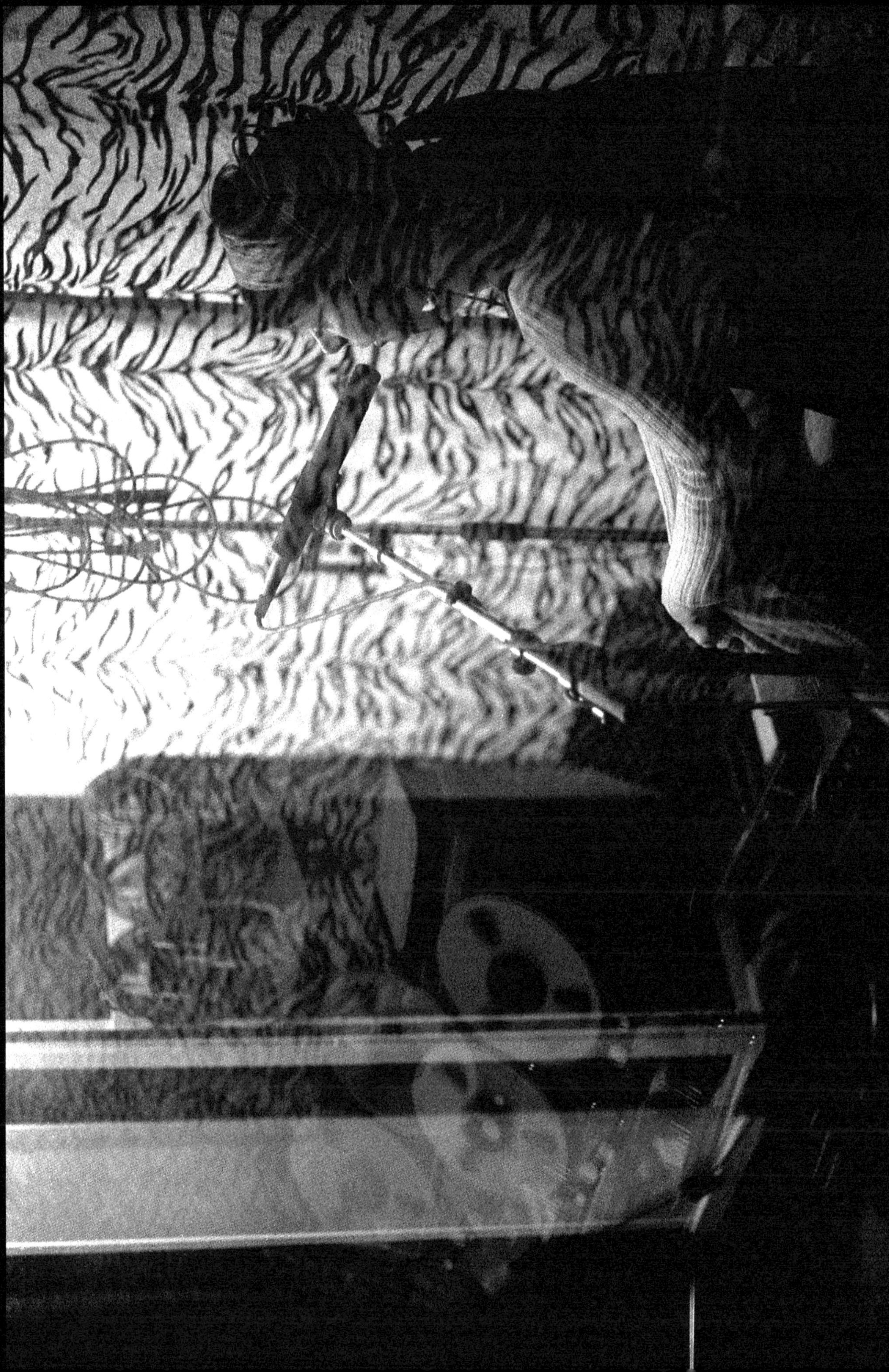

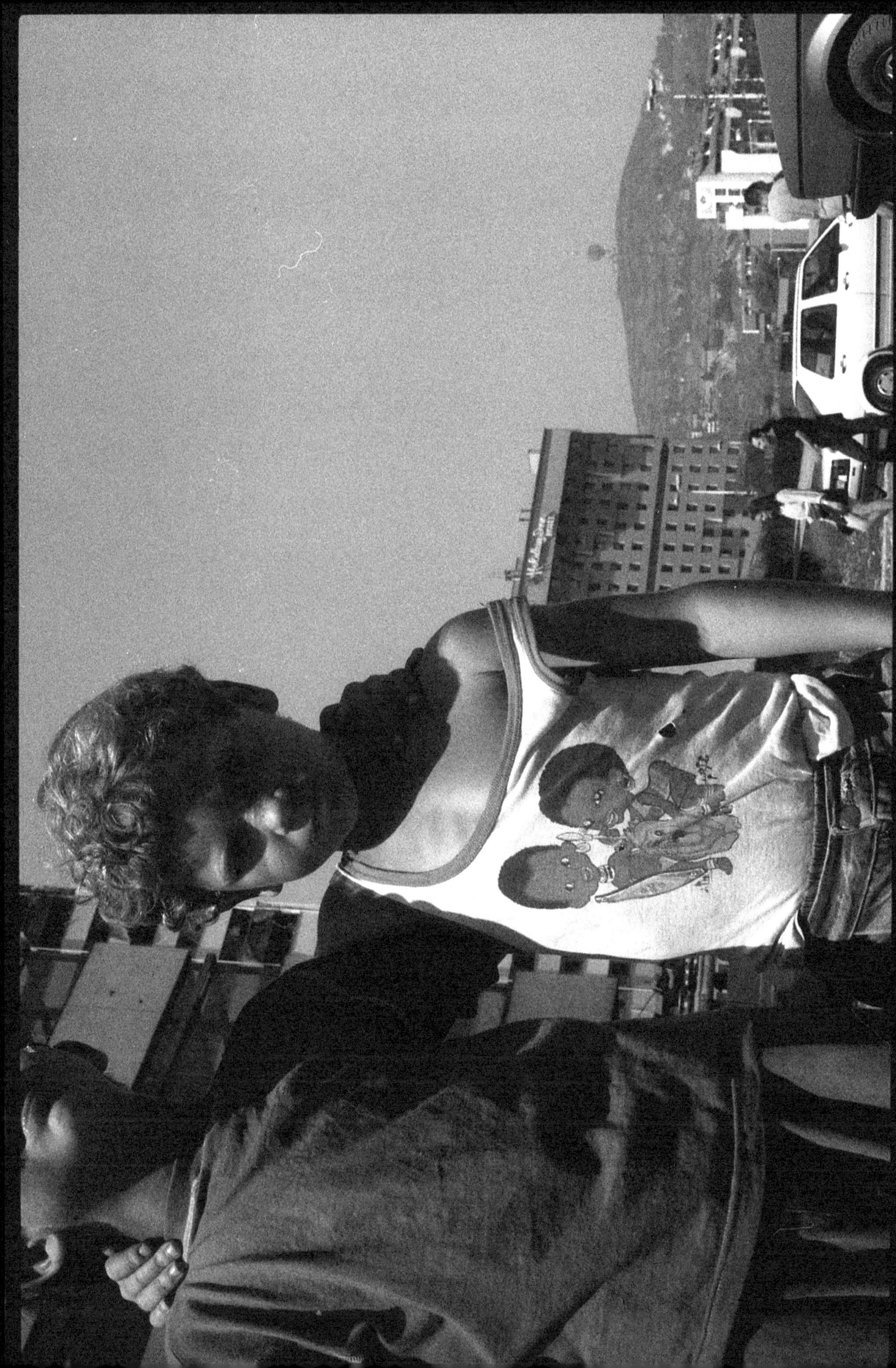

KANSAS

Venezuela
Pampero
Matusalem
Guatemala
Ron Zacapa Centenario

CON
WITH
BUS

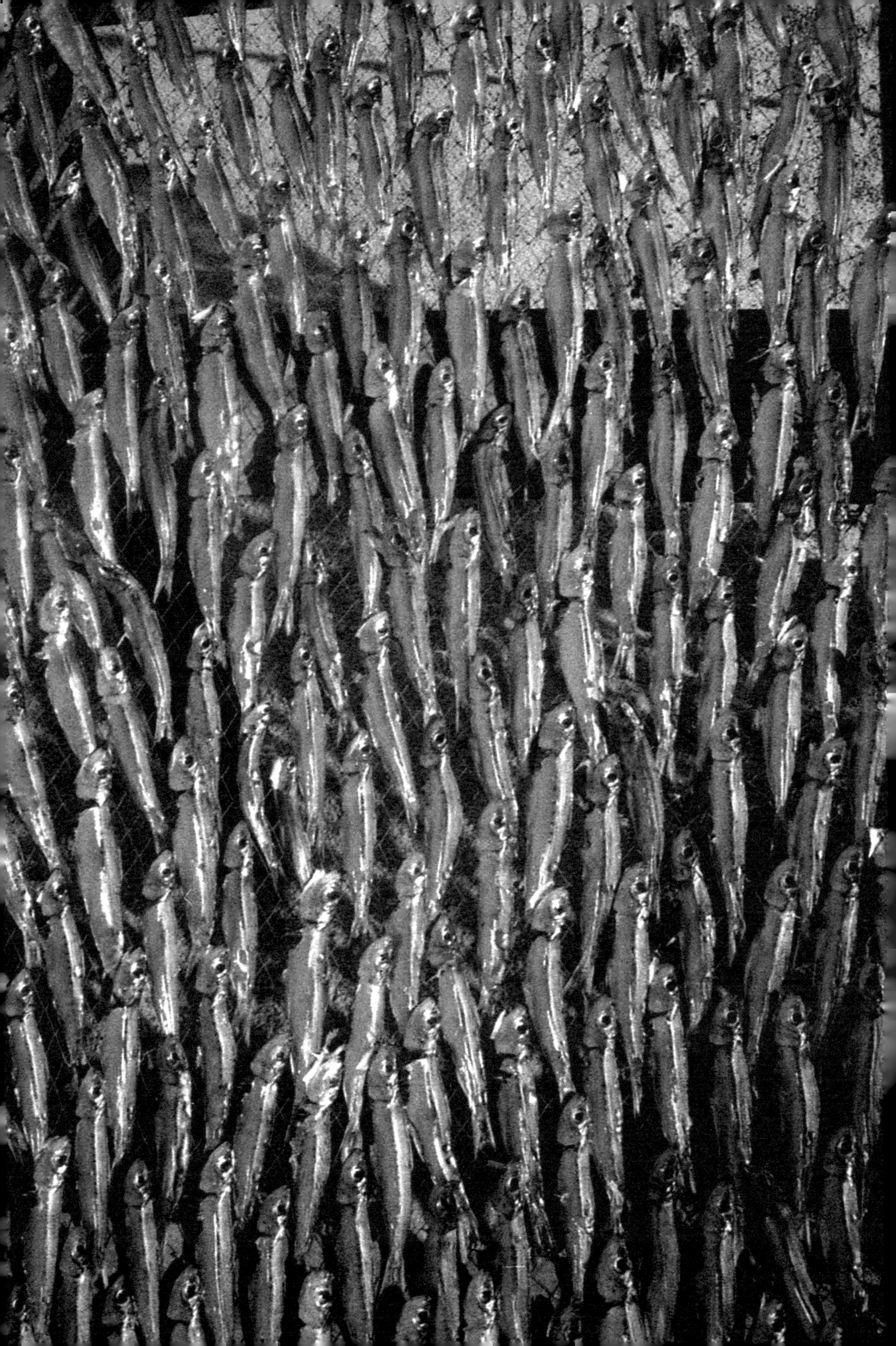

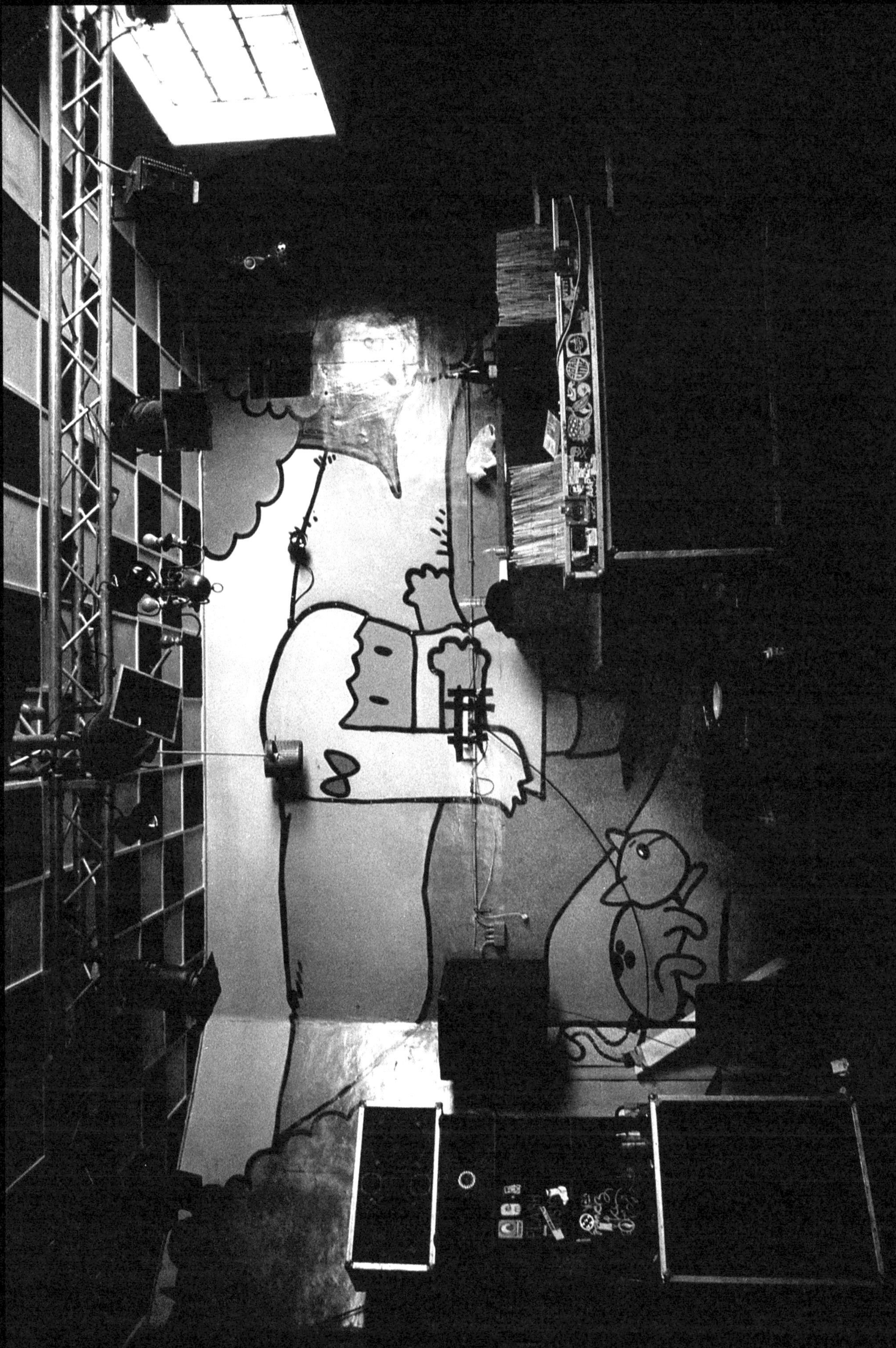

Jupiler

52
50

FATKAT records
VOETGANGERS HIER OVERSTEKEN

HOTEL

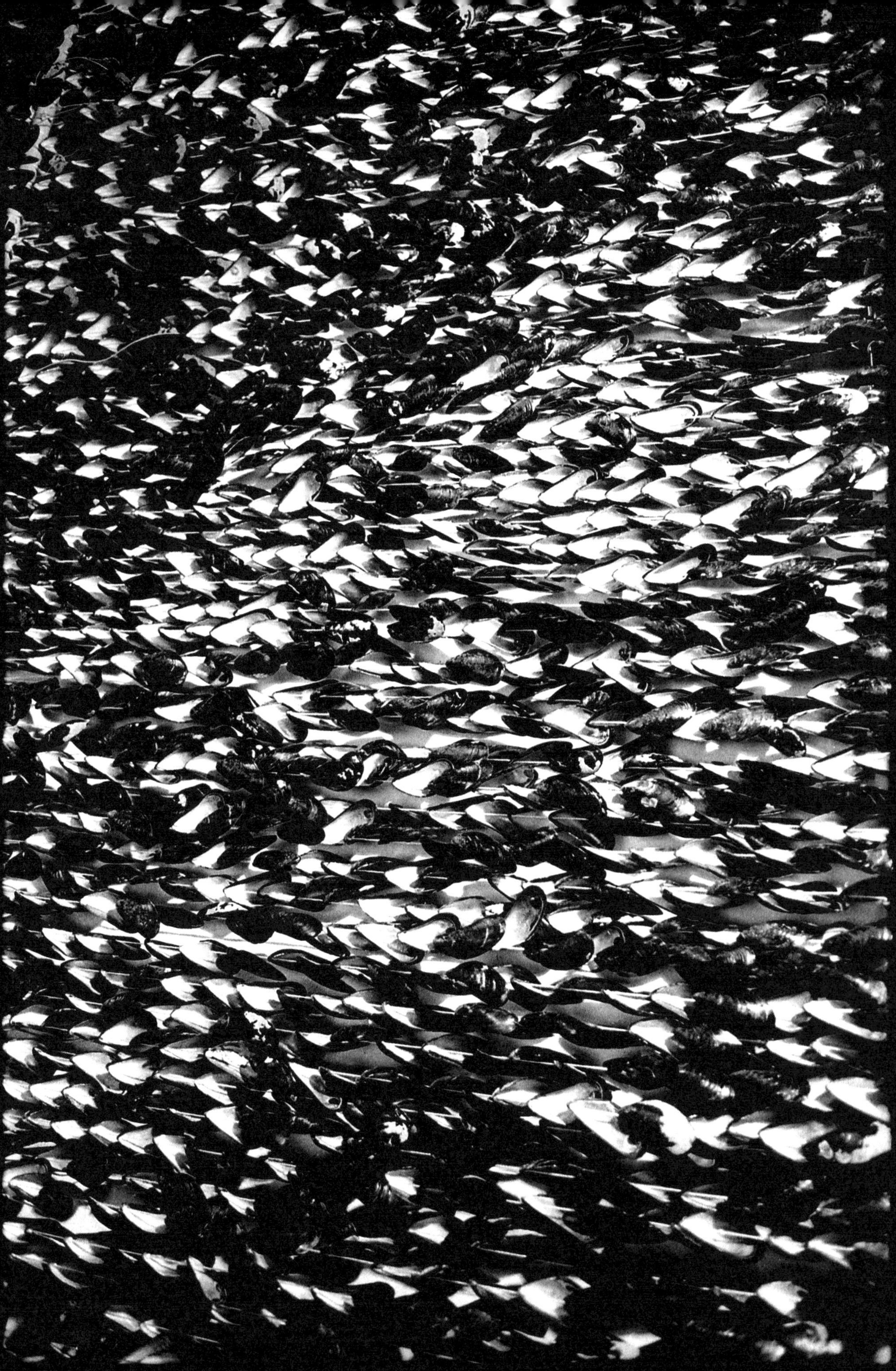

69 parsons

PLEASE USE THE OTHER DOOR
HET BOS
courtisane festival

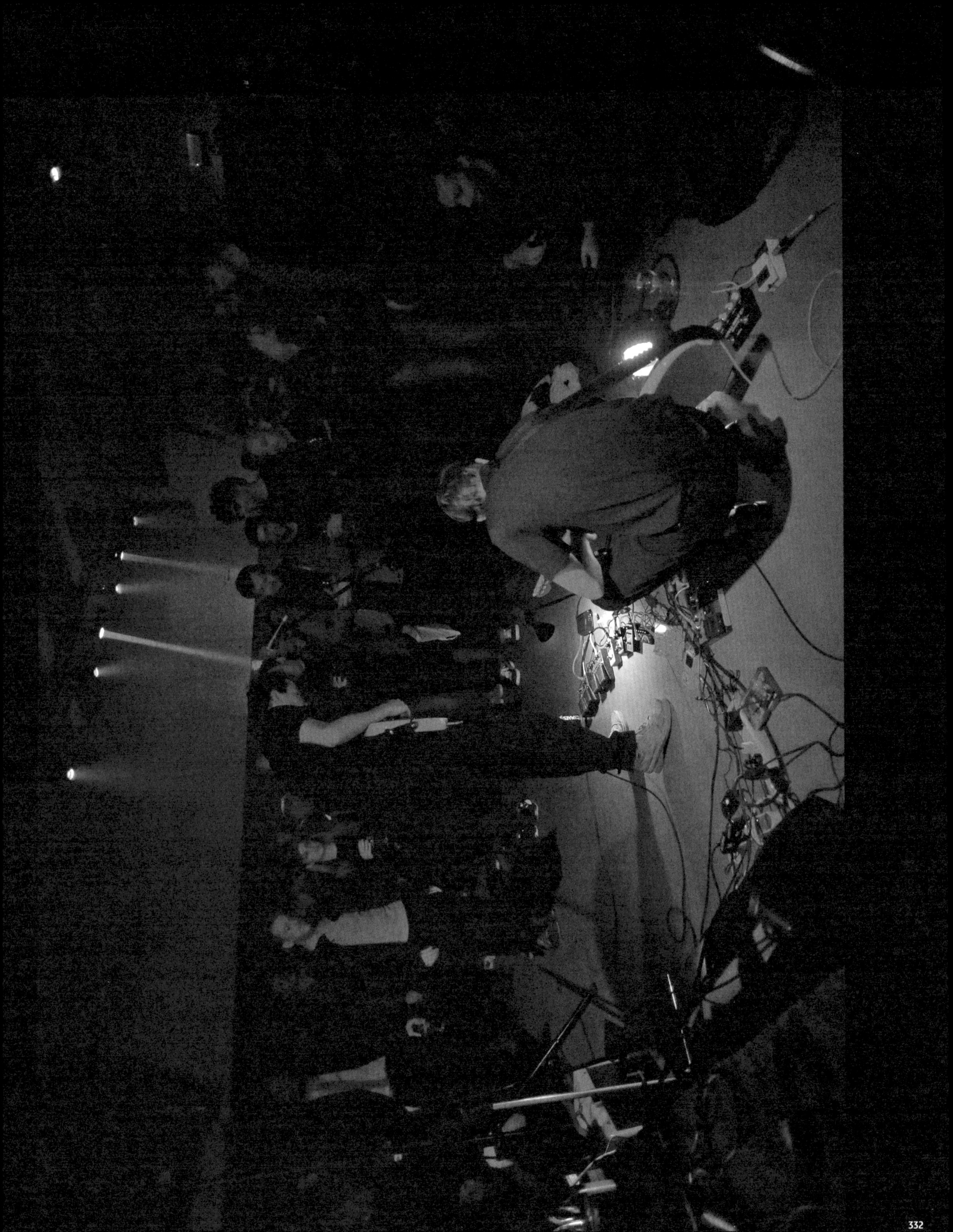

Een dagelijks pad geplaveid met tegels die wij
vaak niet meer registreren. Jij lichtte ze op
en ontdekte een klein universum.
De muziek, de plekken in de stad of wat verder weg.
Mensen vinden die door jou gevonden wilden worden.
De taal van de authenticiteit is universeel.
Daar waren vaak niet veel woorden voor nodig.
Beelden gelukkig des te meer.
En nu is er het boek. Om daar een jongere versie
van mezelf terug te vinden in een smetteloze
verschijning op de laatste dag van 1996 ergens
in Praag. Tussen een verzameling met
momenten waar ik niet aanwezig was.
En ik had er ook bij kunnen zijn, zonder twijfel.
Want het zijn vaak de scènes waar je ook
een rol had willen spelen. Of liever gezegd
welkom bent.
Onmiskenbaar woont de muziek ook in deze
hoek. Een onuitputtelijke bron.
En wat ligt er veel te verstoffen.
Deze ruime verzameling aan klanken en
beelden, daar werden we jaarlijks op
getrakteerd. Of we wilden of niet.
En natuurlijk wilden wij dat.
Nog steeds.

Edmond Steinbusch, May 2024

Mark Rietveld Photographer 1969–2022

Self-portrait, August 18th 2014

57 Room Tramsingel, Breda, 1994
58 Rosa Wissant, France, 1995
59 Paris
60 Tenace Orchestra, Het Bos Antwerp, March 2015
61 Dans dans playing in Witzli-Poetzli Antwerp, April 2011
62 On the road with Marien
63 Sarajevo, 1998
64 Kaboom Karavan, café Kiebooms Antwerp, 2011
65 Kaboom Karavan, café Kiebooms Antwerp, 2011
66 Prague, Czech Republic, 1992/1993
67 End of Queen's Day Amsterdam, 1995
68 Portugal
69 Poetry with Marien in Arnhem, the Netherlands, 1995
70 Rinke's van
71 Sarajevo, 1998
72 Miaux plays in Base-Alpha Gallery Antwerp, 2011
73 Tenace Orchestra, Het Bos Antwerp, March 2015
74 Het Zwin, close to Knokke, November 2020
75 Ruben Machtelinckx and Frederik Leroux in the garden of Het Bos, July 2018
76 Simon and Wessel arriving from Italy on their Puch-mopeds, Schapenstraat Antwerp, 2015
77 Simon and Wessel arriving from Italy on their Puch-mopeds, Schapenstraat Antwerp, 2015
78 Party people Queen's Day Amsterdam, 1995
79 Tacheles Berlin, 1992
80 Karen Elson, 2014
81 De Kift, 1995
82 Mauro in front of Tune Up Records Antwerp, 2008
83 Party, Cologne, 1995
84 Snowman Antwerp, December 2009

85 Mauwkie sleeping in the drum kit
86 Café 't Half Souke Antwerp, December 2011
87 Mark & Janneke on a wedding, 1997
88 Living room in Tabor, Czech Republic, 1998
89 Olympic Stadium Berlin, 1991
90 Puch-meeting, 1990
91 Puch-meeting Breda, early morning 1990
92 El Hafrado plays in Witzli-Poetzli Antwerp, October 2011
93 De Muziekdoos, Antwerp, 1994
94 Flying Horseman plays in Witzli-Poetzli, Antwerp
95 Janneke, winter 2011
96 Reichstag Berlin, 1992
97 Antwerp, 1999
98 Nick Cave, Pukkelpop Kiewit Hasselt, 1990
99 Nick Cave, Pukkelpop Kiewit Hasselt, 1990
100 Ultra Eczema's Dienstplicht: The Space Lady, Het Bos Antwerp, 2014
101 Bar à Bas, Antwerp, 2011
102 On the road with Edmond
103 Cottage with many toilets, Ruige Heide, 2021
104 Mme Belga & Rose, Tenace Rupelmonde, 2020
105 Radio Centraal, broadcasting from La Campine Antwerp, 2009
106 Scheld'apen under the trees Antwerp, 2001
107 Benjamin and Mario, Antwerp, 2009
108 Mad Professor, Het Bos Antwerp, November 2015
109 The Country Kittens, minigolf Beatrijs, Antwerp, 2021
110 With Puch-mopeds to a music festival
111 Elko B., Fatkat Record Store Day Antwerp, 2011
112 Still life in Prague, 1993

113 Edmond, Breda, 1998

114 Prague

115 River Scheldt, Antwerp

116 Flying Horseman, basement session Antwerp, 2011

117 Nieuw Zwart Trio, Tenace Antwerp, 2012

118 Eric Thielemans, Wintervuur Antwerp, January 2012

119 Rudy Trouvé, Coffee & Vinyl Antwerp, 2014

120 Bad Boys at Factor 44 Antwerp, 2015

121 Mother and daughter, Miepie and Pipas, Schapenstraat Antwerp, 2015

122 Frans Van Isacker, 2015

123 Suzuki Junzo, Audioplant (Bar à Gauche), Left Bank Antwerp, 2012

124 Snow, Jura, 2010

125 Sexa, Zanetti Breda, 1993

126 Berlin, Edmond sleeping, 1992

127 River Scheldt at night

128 Janneke and Mark, Schapenstraat Antwerp, 2009

129 Audience for Ben Miroko, Steenhouwersvest Antwerp, 2012

130 Jan Matthé, Café De Vuilen Hond, Fort 8 Hoboken Antwerp, 2011

131 Fred Bervoets, Permeke Library Antwerp, March 2018

132 Rurik & Basho, Tenace Antwerp, 2012

133 Ruisbestuivingen, Dok Ghent, 2011

134 Het Bos Antwerp, February 2016

135 Horse, Breda

136 Snow walk Rivierenhof Antwerp, 2021

137 Charles Bridge over the Vltava, Prague, 1997

138 El Hafrado, January 2015

139 In front of Het Bos Antwerp, October 2018

140 Ludo Mich and Chantal in M HKA Antwerp, 2011

141 Hands, Schapenstraat Antwerp, 2021

142 Strangelove, Antwerp, March 2012

143 Plants, Schapenstraat Antwerp, 2021

144 Warre Fungus and Sam, Audioplant (Bar à Gauche), Left Bank Antwerp, 2012

145 Ina in the car

146 Willis Earl Beal, AB Brussels, 2013

147 Willis Earl Beal, AB Brussels, 2013

148 Mittland Och Leo, Werkkamp in Fort 8 Hoboken Antwerp, 2011

149 Rose & Orry, the best helmsmen are on shore, Merksem Antwerp, 2015

150 The terrace across Portugal, 2003

151 Guy Rombouts, Mme Belga & de Willy on the Tenace, Antwerp, summer 2013

152 Thurston Moore, AB Brussels, 2007

153 Thurston Moore, Scheld'apen Antwerp, March 2012

154 Mme Belga on het boat Tenace, Houtdok Antwerp, summer 2014

155 On the road with Roel QoQo's sandwich 'Indianapolis', 1991

156 Bent Vande Sompele at home, Antwerp, 2014

157 Bar Paniek Antwerp, 2021

158 Scheld'apen crew, Antwerp, 2012

159 Corona wanderings, boat trip out of Amsterdam, 2020

160 Little dog in Tabor, Czech Republic, 1998

161 Cocaine Piss, Het Bos Antwerp, March 2016

162 Carnaval, Giny's house in Breda, 1994

163 Meeting Puch-mopeds in Breda, June 2009

164 Bert Dockx with Dans Dans, Trix Antwerp, 2012

165 Elton in the kitchen, Schapenstraat Antwerp, 2007

166 Kim Peers, Scheld'apen Antwerp, February 2012

167 Dennis Tyfus & Jan Matthé at 'Stockholm', Antwerp, 2014

168 Cato, 1994

169 Centro sociale occupato, Italy, 1991

170 Camping site with Puch-mopeds

171 Self-portrait, Tramsingel Breda, 1995

172 Guillaume Bijl, Forward in time, 15 years of Ultra Eczema, LLS387 Antwerp, 2012

173 Escape-Ism, February 2018

174 Dennis Tyfus, Mima Schwahn & Vaast Colson in front of Stadslimiet, summer 2012

175 Cassettes, Het Bos Antwerp, 2014

176 Orry in the spotlight, Tenace Antwerp, 2014

177 Café Kiebooms, Antwerp, 2015

178 Cato, 1994

179 Ignatz, Tenace Antwerp, 2012

180 Café Atlas, Antwerp, 1992

181 Café De Kat, Antwerp, 2010

182 Erwin Van Looveren's drawing machine, Het Bos Antwerp, October 2018

183 Erwin Van Looveren's drawing machine, Het Bos Antwerp, October 2018

184 Dierck, master of ceremonies, 2015

185 Jan, Bar Paniek Antwerp, 2020

186 Daniel Higgs Scheld'apen Antwerp, 2007

187 Daniel de Botanicus, La Campine Antwerp, 2009

188 Self-portrait, De Nor Antwerp, 2021

189 Rudy Trouvé & Elko Blijweert on the Left Bank Antwerp, 2012

190 Carnaval in Zanetti Breda, 1996

191 Album cover for 'Jeugdzonden' with Giny & Inge, 1995

192 Kogumaza, Scheld'apen Antwerp, 2011

193 Joyce and Matou, Tilburg

194 Jozef Van Wissem, Scheld'apen Antwerp, 2012

195 Suzanne, Zanetti Breda

196 Miguel, La Campine Antwerp, 2009

197 Puchs, Bergen op Zoom

198 France, 1991

199 Roosendaal

200 Drinking brothers, Warsaw, Poland, 1993

201 Rudy Trouvé & Lou Barlow, Trix Antwerp, October 2015

202 Daniel Higgs in Gunther Antwerp, 2012

203 Students' protests, Amsterdam, 1994

204 Puch-meeting in squatted church in Breda, 1995

205 Het Bos, February 2018

206 Greg's trailer, Scheld'apen Antwerp, 2001

207 Janneke and Nop at a wedding in Breda, 1997

208 Café De Vuilen Hond, Fort 8 Hoboken Antwerp, 2011

209 Kalmthoutse Heide, 2021

210 Tenace Charleroi, summer 2014

211 Jeffrey Lee Pierce, Breda, 1994

212 Barcelona, 1996

213 Capsule 'Kartonnen Jubileum', Het Bos Antwerp, February 2017

214 Krakow, Poland, 2011

215 Rudy Trouvé Septet, Antwerp, March 2009

216 Tom Cora plays with The Ex, 1994

217 Looking at the machines of Remörk, Het Bos Antwerp, June 2019

218 Flying Horseman, Trix Antwerp, 2011

219 Party, Cologne, 1995

220 Benjamin-bird, part of the Kalender09-project, Antwerp, 2009

221 Ferdi, Adjan & Roos, garden of the squatted church in Breda, 1995

222 Arjan & Floris, Antwerp

223 Traktor playing on the Meir Antwerp, 2003

224 Jawa, Czech Republic

225 Carlo of Tune Up Records Antwerp, 2008

226 Prague early morning, 1995

227 Telespargel, Berlin, 2003

228 Floor & Mike, Antwerp, 2011

229 Zita Swoon, Antwerp, 1998

230 Flying Horseman

231 Damo Suzuki & Benny Boogers at 'Stockholm', Antwerp, 2014

232 Granada, Spain, 1996

233 Ludo and Chantal, the loudest laugh of the planet, Factor 44 Antwerp, 2015

234 Body/Head Scheld'apen Antwerp, February 2012

235 First apartment in a new town, Antwerp, 1998

236 Serbia, 2003

237 Noorderwijk with the moped

238 Looking and listening to Baudouin Oosterlynck, Stadslimiet, 2012

239 Tune Up Records Antwerp, 2008

240 Noorderwijk with a typewriter

241 Rose and her garden in Rupelmonde, spring 2021

242 Rudy Trouvé, Coffee & Vinyl Antwerp, 2014

243 The Tone Zones, Het Bos Antwerp, 2015

244 Antwerp

245 Fishermen, Lagos, Portugal

246 Janneke & cat

247 Second house in Antwerp, 1999

248 Muddy Decibell

249 The Ex, 1994

250 DJ Guillaume Bijl, Audioplant (Bar à Gauche), Left Bank Antwerp, 2013

251 Ferdi, Zanetti Breda, 1996

252 Edmond and Arjan preparing for a raft trip, Breda, 1993

253 Cycling in Breda, 1996

254 Black Sea hotel lobby, Varna, Bulgaria, 2007

255 Café Pelikaan Antwerp

256 Sad song with Arjan, Breda, 1991

257 Arjan and Ina, Breda, Christmas 1993

258 Exhibition on the floor

259 Preparation for an exhibition, Ten Oosten, 1997

260 Kati

261 Giny, recordings in Amsterdam, 1993

262 On the way to Rupelmonde, spring 2021

263 Sisters Inge & Giny and Dorien, Zanetti Breda, 1992

264 Sarajevo, 1998

265 Sarajevo, 1998

266 Daniel de Botanicus, LLS387 Antwerp, November 2022

267 Greg, Dennis & Kati

268 Sleepy Cats, Schapenstraat Antwerp, 2015

269 Adjan and Hedwig sleeping in the night train, Czech Republic, 1996

270 Budapest, 1996

271 Dans Dans playing in Witzli-Poetzli Antwerp, April 2011

272 Tenace Orchestra, Het Bos Antwerp, March 2015

273 Tenace Orchestra, Het Bos Antwerp, March 2015

274 Sonia con/with garage, Granada, Spain, 1996

275 Alhambra, Granada, Spain, 1996

276 Bedroom Tramsingel Breda

277 Bedroom Tramsingel Breda

278 Laundry, Toruń, Poland, 1993

279 Caravan hiding, Antwerp

280 Nathan Bowles, Bar à Bas Antwerp, 2011

Mark initially began traveling on vintage Puch mopeds, a lifestyle we shared.
In this context, he challenged us in 1993 to race from Breda to Paris, spanning 500 kilometers on these 50cc engines. It was in Paris that he once boldly declared *Serendipity* to be his favorite word: 'The fact of something interesting or pleasant happening by chance'. Little did I know, yet he expected us to have our own, equally thoughtful, response ready. Interestingly, during that first rally, on the French border, they were enjoying some sunny grass as we flew by, cleverly overtaking them. Seemingly surprised, he whipped out his camera and snapped the winning shot. We did win that race.

In nightlife's embrace, Mark stumbled upon souls who mirrored his own. Convinced of the inherent beauty within each being, he sought out those pristine details and resonant sounds appearing to be still. In the raw beauty of everyday life, on society's edges, amidst crowds, on or beside stages, he aimed to capture the essence through his lens, often discovering its own world within. In a still image, he was able to transform the ordinary into the extraordinary and weave entire stories into a single frame.

Often, while enjoying the spoils of life together, Mark would treat us to his vast collection of images and sounds. They were full of serendipities. They still are.

Dierck Roosen, May 2024

Dear Mark,
Some time ago, I started walking and wandering through your archives with the intention of making a book with your work. It feels like you observe the world from a sort of stillness and always with a lot of love. Thank you for sharing your mind's eye with us. I must say it was a very beautiful but not that easy journey when leafing through your archives, because many (personal) emotions and experiences came to the surface — trembling. It was an intense encounter to get into this intimate dialogue with you. And you know, during the making process of this book I lost two good friends of mine which got me more and more confronted with the (perhaps, existential) question: "How to keep something alive?" Yes, how to continue a conversation with our 'Grateful Dead'... with our beloved 'ghosts'? Indeed... and see here, a book by Mark Rietveld! Looking... reading your work felt like eating!

Thanks a lot for this gift.
We plan a new meeting next week — ok?

Hugs, Nico, May 2024

Photography: Mark Rietveld
Editing: Nico Dockx, Janneke Hertoghs
Texts: Nico Dockx, Dierck Roosen, Edmond Steinbusch
Design: David Boon, Nico Dockx
Printing: Zwartopwit
Publisher: Bruno Devos at HOPPER&FUCHS
Prints: Stijn Buyst, Sara Anke Morris, Simon Van Steenis
ISBN: 9789464002416

With support of Stadscowboy vzw, ArchiVolt / Royal Academy of Fine Arts Antwerp

A LONG LOVING LOOK

Thanks to everyone, to all the friends, all the night owls and crowds, all the musicians and artists, to everyone who organized all the beautiful concerts and happenings, especially to everyone who organized, performed, cooked, the Puch mopeds, cleaned up after, to the Verenigde Toilet Madammen, to everyone who was there and all the people that could not come on the 18th of August 2022 to make Mark's farewell a wonderful evening. Thanks to everyone who appeared in front of Mark's camera and supported to make this book.

Thank you Mark.